THE ART OF STARVATION

SHEILA MACLEOD
THE ART OF STARVATION

A STORY OF ANOREXIA AND SURVIVAL

SCHOCKEN BOOKS · NEW YORK

First American edition published by Schocken Books 1982
10 9 8 7 6 5 4 3 2 1   82 83 84 85
Copyright © Sheila MacLeod 1981
Published by agreement with Virago Ltd., London

Library of Congress Cataloging in Publication Data
MacLeod, Sheila.
The art of starvation. A story of anorexia and survival.
Includes bibliographical references.
1. Anorexia nervosa—Patients—United States—Biog-
graphy. 2. MacLeod, Sheila. I. Title.
RC552.A5M3 1982   616.85'2   81-16597
AACR2

Designed by Jackie Schuman
Manufactured in the United States of America
ISBN 0–8052–3803–4

CONTENTS

INTRODUCTION

At this moment, it is estimated that in this country, 1 in every 200 adolescent girls is starving herself—possibly to death. For girls over 16 in the private sector of education or for young women in university populations, the figure can be as high as 1 in 100. Of these, about 15 in every 100 will actually die.[1] Of the remainder, only half will recover to lead more or less normal lives: the rest are likely to relapse, or resort to alternating bouts of feasting and fasting, or, at best, to go through life waging a never-ceasing struggle with their own bodies in order to maintain an "ideal" weight which is barely above the danger-line. The figures, based on previous studies, are startling, but even so they probably underestimate the prevalence of the mysterious and crippling psychosomatic disorder known as anorexia nervosa. It is variously described as a food phobia, a weight phobia, "a fear of all that is involved in growing-up and achieving physical maturation,"[2] a death-wish, a denial of sexuality and gender, or, more popularly, "the slimming disease." Although there is some truth in some of these ascriptions, others of them are misleading and none, in itself, is particularly enlightening. Certainly they do not add up to a coherent picture of the disease and, despite the fact that it is becoming more and more common,[3] there is still a great deal of disagreement and confusion in the medical and psychiatric establishments as to what it actually is. With some notable exceptions, the emphasis has generally been on the negative, destructive aspects of the disease, on the "unnatural" aversion to what the rest of us like to call the good things in life—food, sex, maturity, conviviality, and so on. But, as I hope to demonstrate, this is only half the story, only one half of the total paradox which constitutes anorexia nervosa.

What is now clear are the clinical criteria for the diagnosis of the disease—at least in its most obvious, medical aspects. The most noticeable symptom is, of course, a major weight loss. By the time an anorexic gets to see a doctor or a psychiatrist, she may have lost as much as 40 to 55 pounds over a period of nine months to two years. In extreme cases she will have lost around 50 percent of her previous body weight. There will be no apparent organic reason for the loss, and so the clinician is likely to direct her/his attention to the patient's wholesale resistance to fattening foods—a category which eventually expands (or has already expanded) to include all food whatsoever. Resistance can take the form of downright refusal to eat, excuses for non-eating—such as lack of appetite or sheer inability—the secret disposal or destruction of food, self-induced vomiting or excessive purging. At the same time the patient will display an obsessive interest in food, in some cases insisting on cooking for and overfeeding her own immediate family. It has been shown that when weight has been drastically reduced, menstruation will cease, and that this generally happens when the patient's weight falls to below 98 pounds.[4] Amenorrhoea is therefore another universal symptom of anorexia nervosa. On closer physical examination, it is likely that the anorexic will be found to be suffering from constipation, cold blue extremities, slow heart beat (bradycardia), low blood pressure (hypotension), and a low basal metabolic rate. All these symptoms can be described as general effects of starvation. A more exhaustive examination is likely to reveal some, if not all, of its secondary effects: abnormal glucose tolerance levels, high carotene and cholesterol levels in the blood, fluctuations in water balance, and a low output of sex hormones. She may also have grown some downy hair on normally hairless parts of her body. But at the same time she will have retained her pubic and armpit hair as well as the shape of her breasts, and so glandular insufficiency must be ruled out as the root cause of her symptoms. In fact, after even the most exhaustive tests, no physiological causes at all will be found to account for her extreme and seemingly inexplicable weight loss.

In spite of this overall clinical picture, she will deny that there is anything wrong with her, either physically or emotionally, insisting against all appearances to the contrary that she is well and happy and, above all, not thin to the point of emaciation. As if in proof of the superior truth of her own point of view, she may evince an unnatural brightness which will turn out to be only a part of a larger pattern of hyperactivity. Or she may be quiet and polite, at pains to give the impression that, although there is really nothing to worry about, she will do all she can to cooperate with the doctor and her parents in the attempt to restore her to her normal weight. In short, she will lie—in word or deed or in both at once. The true assertion that she could be starving herself to death will be greeted with disbelief, if not scorn, and she will assert in turn that her weight loss is only a temporary aberration which she will rectify of her own accord. It will soon become clear to the clinician that she has no intention of modifying her behavior and, if treatment proceeds, it will also become clear that, despite all assurances to the contrary, she will use every trick she can devise with the unswerving determination of an addict, to avoid any such modification. She will cling to her disease, seemingly indifferent to its possibly fatal results and to its devastating effects on others who are concerned with her health and well-being.

The anorexic's behavior is puzzling and eventually becomes infuriating to those around her, who are reduced to helplessness in the face of her intransigence. She wounds those nearest her by rejecting all they have to offer her. To them, her persistent refusal to eat seems like the epitome of perversity: she is choosing death rather than life, sickness rather than health or, at best, a narrow existence in preference to a full one. They can see no reasons for her behavior. But of course there are reasons, many of them too close to home to be seen by those involved. I think I know what some of those reasons are. I suffered myself from anorexia nervosa for some eighteen months just over twenty years ago when I was sixteen to seventeen years old, and I have had two minor relapses since. Because the disease was rarer (and certainly more rarely mentioned) in those days, it was not recognized for what it was by any of the adults—parents, teachers, even doctors—who had reason to question why I was losing weight so rapidly, and I received no treatment, although I was scolded a great deal and frequently told to "snap out of it." At the onset of the disease I weighed 117 pounds, and was five feet two-and-a-half inches tall. Like the majority of anorexics, I was not exactly obese but only slightly and quite suddenly overweight. However, I made no conscious decision to diet and, although I did not particularly like the way I looked—a common enough attitude in adolescent girls—it did not worry me unduly. I never connected my refusal of food with the desire to be slim and, by definition, sexually attractive. I didn't know what I was doing: I just felt compelled to do it. All the same, when I had lost 14 pounds I felt I had achieved something and was determined to go on to greater heights of achievement. Eventually, my weight dropped to 78 pounds. It was at this point that my spontaneous recovery began. But it wasn't until two years later that I first heard the phrase "anorexia nervosa," when it was applied to a fellow-student in whom I recognized—with some horror—the image of my former self: a pathetically emaciated creature whose head seemed too large for her body, and who seemed to be in a permanent state of shivering and shrinking away from everything. Until then I could have been, for all I knew, the only person in the world ever to have behaved as I had behaved or felt as I had felt. And it was many years later still that I discovered not only my physical symptoms but also my state of mind to have been almost entirely typical of the syndrome of primary anorexia nervosa.

It was only then that I began to question the whole phenomenon in depth. In doing so I have found myself in frequent disagreement with others who have written on the subject. The relevant literature is all based on clinical experience and written from the point of view of the clinician or therapist who has necessarily been forced into making generalizations from the available data. My aim in this book is to particularize, to tell my own story, and at the same time relate it to the findings of those who have dealt with anorexics as patients. In my experience, anorexia nervosa is not a matter of slimming which has somehow or other got out of hand and beyond the control of the anorexic herself. Neither does it signify an urge towards suicide, nor yet an aversion from sexuality. On the contrary, it is, like most other psychoneurotic syndromes, a positive strategy aimed at establishing autonomy and resolving what would otherwise be unbearable conflicts in the life of the sufferer. These conflicts are partially related to and arising from the anorexic's individual history and personality structure —that is, they are intrapsychic. But they are also existential, that is, related to being-in-the-world, which for human beings necessarily means being-in-a-body, and for women, being-in-a-female-body.

I have decided to meet the phenomenon in meeting my former self and attempting to recall what was actually going on both before the onset of the disease and during the time that it was taking its course. I was trying to resolve something, trying to prove something and, through the language of my symptoms, to say something. Whether she knows it or not, and however obliquely metaphorical the language of her symptoms may appear, the anorexic is trying to tell us something, and something quite specific about herself and the context in which she exists. We know, from the outside, that it is something of tremendous importance because some anorexics would rather die than stop saying it. We know too, that it concerns being a girl and being a woman, and the passage from the one to the other, because anorexia nervosa is typically confined to teenage girls and young women. And because the disease is becoming more common, extending itself through all strata of society instead of being largely confined to the upper- and middle-classes, we must assume that what is being said is becoming increasingly important to increasing numbers of people. After a brief outline of the documented history of the disease, I should like to explore and try to explain, from the inside, what I believe this something to be.

1
GENERAL HISTORY

Anorexia nervosa has probably been with us for hundreds of years. It has been suggested that the disease was not uncommon in the Middle Ages among women who were said to be possessed by the devil and persecuted as witches. I find this plausible for two reasons. Witches were always female (as were the hysterics treated by Freud, who himself drew an explicit parallel between the two[1]), they were also often healers, dispensers of simples and potions to the poor, and especially to poor women. In other words, they were identified by their persecutors as people who at once displayed hysterical behavior and professed to have control over the human body. The anorexic's symptoms have often been described as hysterical, and the notion that she has complete control over her own body is her prime delusion. But there is another and perhaps more cogent connection between anorexics and witches. Some witches were neither hysterical nor deluded, but were persecuted either at random or because of their medical knowledge, especially of midwifery. In the latter cases they were especially resented and feared by the male-dominated religious establishments, who claimed to have a monopoly of all knowledge and to whom the female body was, according to the traditional Judaeo-Christian view, a mysterious, unpredictable and even evil thing unless it were kept in its proper place and confined to its proper roles: chastity or incessant childbearing within marriage.[2] Similarly today the prevalent view of the female body is male-oriented and its care largely in the hands of male-dominated medical and psychiatric establishments. But the male view of the female body does not necessarily coincide with a woman's perception of her own body. In fact, the two can be entirely at odds. It is this very conflict which is, in my opinion, one of the major factors in the genesis (aetiology) of anorexia nervosa.

The first identification of the disease has generally been credited to Richard Morton, an English physician who published his *Phthisologia: or a Treatise on Consumption* in 1689. He referred to the condition as a "nervous consumption," but from his two detailed case histories, in which he described such symptoms as amenorrhoea, constipation and hyperactivity co-existing with extreme emaciation and indifference on the part of the patient towards both her condition and cure, it is clear that what he was describing was anorexia nervosa. The connection and confusion with "consumption" are both interesting. Even today a young person who suddenly loses a lot of weight is likely to be screened and tested (as indeed I was) to exclude the possibility of tuberculosis. Because anorexia nervosa has typically been a disease of the upper or middle classes I am led to wonder how many young ladies of the eighteenth and nineteenth centuries who wasted away or "went into a decline" were not in fact suffering from tuberculosis, which is often associated with poor social conditions, but from anorexia in protest against the narrowness of their social roles and the lack of stimulation in their overprotected lives. I certainly find it difficult to believe, despite the paucity of evidence, that anorexia did not exist during these periods and that there were not emotionally isolated young girls like myself pursuing the same lonely course. In 1875—a year after the anorexia nervosa syndrome had first been defined and isolated—an American doctor, Azell Ames, was stating emphatically that "consumption" in young girls was produced by failure of the menstrual function, although today amenorrhoea is generally seen as a result rather than a cause of tuberculosis. At the time he was writing the disease had reached almost epidemic proportions, and young women were particularly vulnerable, often dying at rates twice as high as men of a similar age.[3] There could be many reasons for this phenomenon, but I suspect that psychological as well as organic factors were at work. I suspect that some of those young women were anorexics.

There is also some contrary evidence to suggest that tuberculosis and anorexia nervosa are mutually exclusive,[4] but I am inclined to doubt this for various reasons. First, I do not see how there can be any relationship of mutual exclusivity between an infectious disease caused by a bacillus and a disease which should more properly be called a psychosomatic disorder. Second, Mara Selvini Palazzoli states that her own cases of advanced anorexia nervosa included one patient who died of acute pulmonary tuberculosis and two who developed tuberculosis but were subsequently cured.[5] Third, the evidence seems to have been based on the observation that anorexics exposed to tuberculosis never contracted the disease while non-anorexics in the same environment (a hospital) became infected. The observation does not surprise me. During the whole time I was anorexic I was never ill with any infectious disease, remaining immune even to colds and flu, while others around me succumbed. Starvation seems to stave off infection. In addition, anorexics tend to have robust physical constitutions: it is one of the facts about themselves which they find intolerable. "Fate," Ellen West wrote in her diary, "wanted me to be heavy and strong, but I want to be thin and delicate."[6] It is also a factor which enables them to maintain their anorexic behavior for so long without collapsing.

In 1789 a French physician, J. Naudeau, published a lengthy description of a fatal case of anorexia nervosa in which he attributed his patient's death to the influence of her mother—a significant attribution because the mother plays a major role in the life of the anorexic. But it was not until the second half of the nineteenth century that the disease was identified as a clinical entity through the simultaneous, but mutually independent, work of E. C. Lasegue, Professor of Clinical Medicine at the University of Paris and W. W. Gull, one of London's most famous and respected surgeons.

Lasegue's paper *On Hysterical Anorexia* was published in April 1873, and claimed that the disease was caused by emotional disturbances which the patient tended to disguise or conceal. He saw the disease as progressive and divided into three distinct phases. The first was said to be characterized by some hysterical disturbance in the digestive system, and a decrease in food intake combined with a marked increase in general activity. The second phase was one of "perversion" in which the patient became obsessed with her own body and its increasing emaciation—an obsession reinforced by the anxiety of her immediate family. The third, or cathectic phase, showed the patient to be suffering from amenorrhoea, constipation, lack of skin elasticity, and to be in a state of depression combined with hyperactivity. Lasegue also noted the patient's indifference to the seriousness of her own condition and her obstinacy in maintaining it. Perhaps more importantly, he emphasized that his description of the disease would be incomplete without reference to the patient's home life: "Both the patient and her family form a tight-knit whole, and we obtain a false impression of the disease if we limit our observation to the patient alone." This approach, with its emphasis on transpersonal relationships, is one which has only recently been taken up again, notably by Mara Selvini Palazzoli in Italy and Salvador Minuchin and others in the United States. Lasegue described in detail, as they were to do later, the interaction between the patient and her family with particular reference to the manner in which the patient's condition gradually came to be the ruling obsession and sole preoccupation of the whole family.

On October 24, 1874, William Gull submitted a paper on anorexia nervosa to the London Clinical Society. Although he had given a series of lectures in 1873 in which he described the disease as "hysteric apepsia," he later insisted that anorexia should be distinguished from hysteria, and it is to him that we owe the term "anorexia nervosa." He stressed that the disease was due to psychopathological factors and listed the outstanding symptoms as emaciation, amenorrhoea, constipation, loss of appetite, slow pulse and respiration, and marked hyperactivity, warning at the same time that compulsive eating—now recognized as an obverse symptom of the disease—sometimes followed a refusal to eat. The patient's behavior was attributed to a "morbid mental state" or to "mental perversity," to which young girls were especially prone. Thus far his description agreed with that of Lasegue, with whose work he was now familiar, recognizing that they had "the same maladie in mind, though the forms of our illustration are different." But whereas Lasegue saw the condition as a "peripheral" disturbance, Gull emphasized its "central origin." Although their two accounts vary as to details and suppositions, they both insisted that anorexia was a mental rather than an organic disease and were at pains to define its psychic genesis. Nevertheless, both diagnosis and treatment have, ever since, been surrounded by controversy and confusion. Much the same arguments as have recently been going on concerning the aetiology of schizophrenia were advanced and rejected and advanced again. Was there a physiological basis to the disease or were its origins purely psychological? By the 1930s it was generally acknowledged that anorexia nervosa was brought about by psychological factors, but there was still no real agreement as to what those factors were. And even today the picture is far from clear.

In 1969 Peter Dally of Westminster Hospital, London, published a monograph on anorexia nervosa in which he sets out the results of his work with a large number of anorexic patients.[7] He was concerned to study the causes of the disease as well as its diagnosis and treatment. According to him, anorexics should be divided into three groups: an "obsessional," a "hysterical," and one of mixed aetiology. The differentiation between the obsessional and the hysteric types seems to have been derived from Pierre Janet, who characterized the latter type as someone who found it impossible to eat, and the former as someone who retained her sense of hunger but refused to eat through a "horror of eating animal flesh, fear of growing fat, of growing-up, of blushing after food, shame and disgust of her body and her still unconquered appetites."[8] I do not find this classification helpful, and Dally's addition of a third category only serves to confuse the issue still further. It seems to me that all cases of anorexia nervosa must necessarily involve both hysterical and obsessional features, and that the separation of the two is based on too-rigid Freudian psychoanalytic thinking. In addition, I find his description of the first two groups as representing primary (or typical or "true") anorexia, while the third group represents the secondary form, quite contrary to my own experience. From the tables given in his book it would appear that Dally's error has been to believe what his patients told him about themselves, ignoring the fact that anorexics are notorious liars. All the same, he has done much to make the anorexic picture clearer in laying down more precise guidelines for both therapy and prognosis, and perhaps most notably in the criteria for assessing improvement and recovery, which seem to have been universally accepted.

With Hilde Bruch's admirable book, *Eating Disorders*,[9] the picture becomes clearer again, if more complex. She too divides anorexia into two forms: primary or typical, and secondary or atypical. Her assignment of patients to the atypical group "is based on the *absence* of the *characteristic features* of the primary syndrome, namely, pursuit of thinness in the struggle for an independent identity, delusional denial of thinness, preoccupation with food, hyperactivity, and striving for perfection." But she is mainly concerned, as I am, with the primary picture. Having worked with anorexics for several decades, she has come to the conclusion that "the non-eating and associated weight loss were late features, secondary to underlying personal disturbance." And in doing so she isolates three areas of disordered psychological functioning.

The first she defines as a "disturbance of delusional proportions in the body image and body concept." The anorexic seems to be genuinely unaware of her true size and, although to others she resembles a skeleton, she will often maintain that she is actually fat. The work of occupational therapists with certain anorexics gives graphic evidence of this particular disturbance.[10] Patients were asked to draw or paint pictures entitled "myself after a meal," and the results invariably showed rotund, shapeless creatures which bore no resemblance to the patients' actual physical appearance at the time. When patients in the same study were asked to depict themselves at target weight—that is, the weight considered to be normal and healthy by the medical authorities —similar pictures emerged. One patient represented herself as a Christmas pudding weighing 124 pounds, and accompanied the painting with the comment "UGH!" Another represented herself as an obese devil, complete with horns and pitchfork, clearly identifying the normal adult female body as both evil and frightening. Yet another drew herself as half a house: the phrase "as big as a house" comes to mind, while the fact that only half of one was represented reveals that the patient saw herself as only half a person at a time when others considered her to be a healthy young woman of normal weight. The implications of such fears and misapprehensions are also discussed by Bruch.

She defines the second area of disordered functioning as a "disturbance of the accuracy of perception or cognitive function or cognitive interpretation of stimuli arising in the body." In other words, the ability to go without sufficient food for months or years on end is less likely to be due to mere loss of appetite (the literal meaning of the word "anorexia") than to the inability to recognize hunger. Hunger pains are often denied, even in the presence of stomach contractions, and the smallest intake of food leads to complaints of acute discomfort. Bruch traces both these delusions to the primary relationship with the mother, and connects the second specifically to a delusion which is also characteristic of obesity. Just as an obese person fails to recognize that she has had enough to eat and goes on eating, so the anorexic fails to recognize that she is not eating enough for her body's needs and stops eating. Eventually, she becomes afraid that, once she starts eating, she, like the obese person, will not be able to stop. In addition to the denial of hunger there is also the denial of fatigue. Anorexics are hyperactive —strangely enough, because the usual symptoms of chronic undernutrition are lassitude and apathy. They tend to indulge in violent and/or prolonged exercise, and it has been shown that they walk an average of 6.8 miles a day compared to the average of 4.0 miles walked by women of normal weight.[11] An anorexic finds it difficult to sit still and difficult to attend to her work, but she will deny these difficulties along with the fatigue which underlies them, and work assiduously, if painfully slowly, determined to get everything right.

The third, and to me the central, area of disordered functioning is described by Bruch as "a paralysing sense of ineffectiveness." The anorexic experiences herself as a passive vessel. Everything she does, even eating (especially eating), is perceived not as an action performed by herself, but as something which happens to her, and over which she consequently has no control. Every action she does take of her own accord is doomed to frustration: it feels like perpetually bashing one's head against a cotton-wool wall. That this deep-seated sense of helplessness should co-exist with hyperactivity and apparent overconfidence is only one of the many paradoxes of anorexia nervosa.

So now the picture has altered slightly. Non-eating is no longer in the foreground and can be seen as a symbolic expression of what is going on within the anorexic's psyche. In her equally admirable book, cited above, Mara Selvini Palazzoli confirms and supports most of Bruch's findings. Her work with anorexics started from an intrapsychic basis, that is, it took the form of individual therapy sessions. From these she arrived at conclusions similar to Bruch's about the anorexic's delusional state and all-pervading sense of helplessness. Like Bruch, she traces these factors to the primary relationship with the mother, and her findings are based on object-relations theory. The anorexic perceives her body as a "thing" distinct from her "self" and so fights it on two planes: as the source of impotence and anxiety because it represents the unacceptable (passive/receptive) part of herself; and as an alien force because she considers it an all-powerful invader of herself. The anorexic

> is prey to a most disastrous Cartesian dichotomy: *she believes that her mind transcends her body* and that it grants her unlimited power over her own behaviour and that of others. The result is a reification of the self and the mistaken belief that the patient is engaged in a victorious battle on two fronts, namely against:
> (1) her body, and
> (2) the family system.[12]

And it is to the family system that Selvini Palazzoli eventually turns her attention. In studying the family as a self-regulating (cybernetic) system, she analyzes the day-to-day functional means of communication (transactional patterns) between its various members and draws attention to those patterns which are characteristic of families with an anorexic member. Such families are generally tight-knit: the parents are outwardly respectable, hard-working, conventional people who do not have rows and show (perhaps excessive) concern for the welfare of their children. But in fact they are people who have repressed their resentment of one another and of their respective roles within the family structure; neither is prepared to assume leadership and claims that all her/his actions are being performed for the good of other members of the family; and each sees any form of alliance or coalition between any other two members of the family as a betrayal of her/himself as well as of the whole system. Transactional rules (often unverbalized or even unconscious) are firmly fixed, and the "rule of rules" is that the rules must not be questioned. These families are highly resistant to change, as they are to any expression of individuality which seems to present the threat of change.

And so Selvini Palazzoli's work with anorexics now tends to consist of family rather than individual therapy. As she explains,

> today we see that the shift from the individual unit posited in psychiatry is but one aspect of a universal cultural shift (in biology, economics, ethology, ecology, etc.), or rather of a new overall calling for the rejection of the study of isolated phenomena in favour of the broader natural context in which these phenomena occur.

This is, of course, a fashionable viewpoint and, when expressed in general terms, there is much to be said in its favor, but I have grave doubts about its specific application to anorexia nervosa. It states that the anorexic's condition is only one manifestation of a malfunctioning family system, and that it is the system as much as the anorexic's own behavior which needs to be changed in order to achieve her full recovery. This may be so in many cases, but it is not the whole story: the anorexic is also an isolated phenomenon. If she were not, if she did not perceive herself as such, she would not be anorexic.

The picture has now changed again, altering its focus considerably. Minuchin and his colleagues also emphasize the importance of the anorexic's immediate family, and more especially its suppressed family conflicts.[13] Dismissing the intrapsychic approach as linear—that is, based on the individual's history of emotional development—and therefore outmoded, they insist on the superior validity of their own systems model. What this means in effect is that they see the current context of the disease as highly significant, more significant perhaps than the aetiology of the patient's inner disturbances. After seven years of investigation, they are prepared to state that the anorexic's family is peculiarly prone to what they call "conflict avoidance": on the surface all is civility, niceness, and loving concern for others; underneath there is anger, resentment, possessiveness, with secrets held between various members of the family to the exclusion of others, and with confidences similarly exchanged and then betrayed. These families are also found to be peculiarly enmeshed and rigid. To them, the family is what matters, is all-important, and the repository of its members' total emotional investment. Individuals tend to speak for one another, to presume to know what the others are thinking and feeling, and to act accordingly. There will be a notable lack of privacy in the family home; and any individual who seeks it will be resented by the others. Minuchin et al. conclude that the anorexic is best treated as a member of a family because her symptoms and her behavior refer not only to her individual psychopathology but to that of the entire family network in which she is enmeshed. Through her disease she has also been speaking for others and, like a scapegoat, has taken the burden of a whole pattern of emotional conflict upon herself.

This model is, of course, very similar to Selvini Palazzoli's latter one as well as to the one formulated by R. D. Laing and others with regard to schizophrenia and schizogenic families. But Minuchin et al. seem to have discarded the intrapsychic approach altogether, along with any consideration of the wider social context emphasized by Selvini Palazzoli, and so for me their model is even less complete than hers. Their therapeutic method often strikes me as being rather brutal and verging upon the behavioristic. And despite their claims as to the large number of cures they have effected, I remain dubious. As Auden put it, "of course Behaviourism works. So does torture. Give me a no-nonsense, down-to-earth behaviourist, a few drugs and simple electronic appliances, and in six months I will have him reciting the Athanasian creed in public."[14] The problems of anorexia nervosa, I restate, lie deep within the individual psyche, and anyone who ignores this fact does so at her/his own peril and at that of the anorexic herself.

Neither can the social and political contexts be ignored. A more recent development in the history of the disease is that exemplified by the feminist approach, which links anorexia nervosa with the social and sexual oppression of women. In particular it emphasizes a woman's relationship with her own body in the context of a male-dominated society. That relationship must necessarily be fraught with all the contradictions apparent in the male attitude to the female body: on the one hand it is an object of idealization and desire; on the other, it is evil and threatening. In short, it is mysterious. But feminists insist that there is no mystery—or, at least, that women's bodies are no more mysterious than men's. They tend to work together as women in self-help groups where anorexics can discuss their symptoms and feelings among themselves and attempt to place them in a wider context than that of the individual's history or the ramifications of relationships within the immediate family.

There are, as I hinted earlier, good historical reasons for this approach. For the last two hundred years or so, the medical professions, like most others, have been dominated by men, and an account of their dealings with their female patients makes horrifying reading.[15] Menstruation, childbirth and female sexuality, as well as the psychoneurotic disturbances characteristic of the nineteenth- and twentieth-century woman, have been treated with scant understanding and sometimes with overt hostility. It is easy to see how an assumption of male superiority on the part of society at large can lead to psychosomatic disorders in an educated female population which has been freed from a round-the-clock drudgery of physical labor, but has not yet been allowed to participate fully and on equal terms with men in the more psychologically satisfying occupations to be pursued outside the home, or the office where an ancillary role is still the norm. And it is easy to see how a similar assumption on the part of the medical profession can serve to exacerbate such disorders: the little woman is patted on the head, given a few pills, and made to feel that she is some sort of "hysterical female" in thus demonstrating her unhappiness or, more accurately, her dissatisfaction with her life. Whether or not this information is of immediate help to the anorexic is another matter, and one to which I shall return.

The picture has become more and more complex. The image of anorexia nervosa has developed from that of an overweight girl who cannot stop dieting, by way of disturbed relationships with others (object-relations) and the Cartesian split cited by Selvini Palazzoli, to that of a microcosm of all our social relations, especially as enacted within the nuclear family or between men and women. When I put myself in the picture, it will be seen that I find some areas of it more valid than others. It will also be seen that I find some truth in each of the approaches described. I cannot base my own approach on collected data, but only on personal experience.

2
BACKGROUND

In examining my own background it seems logical to refer to the findings of Selvini Palazzoli and Minuchin on the families of anorexics, but whereas Minuchin especially confines himself to the family ambience at the time of the onset of the disease, I should like to say a little more about the genesis of that family ambience. Although I agree that "it is always dangerous to assume that the causes of emotional disturbances lie more in the past than the present,"[1] I also know that families, like individuals, in Western societies have histories, and that no two families, happy or unhappy, develop in exactly the same way. In the course of my own childhood and adolescence my immediate family went through several changes, mostly involving separation and loss, but at the same time certain factors remained constant. In fact, it seems to me now that what remained constant did so, and all the more so, because of the changes with which the family was faced. And because the particular form of constancy adopted by my family seems at least as important in the aetiology of my own disease as the changes which accompanied it, I shall start with an anecdote which illustrates, in little, the fixed but complex family structure of which I was a part.

I was about 13 years old, and my aunt (my father's sister) and uncle had come to stay with us—namely, my father, my mother, my four younger sisters and myself. There was nothing unusual in this, visits to and from relatives having been a common feature of my childhood. After lunch one day we went for a walk in the nearby woods, my mother remaining at home with the two younger children and the rest of us accompanying my father and my aunt. It was one of those crisp, clear autumnal days with the leaves vivid and squishy underfoot and the sky above one perfect, if chilling, blue. When the path narrowed, we had to proceed in single file, and I found myself leading the way, with my aunt following closely behind and my father behind her. I was enjoying it all in a mildly responsive sort of way. Then I heard my aunt remark of me to my father, without making any attempt to lower her voice, "She's going to be stout—just like Dolly" (Dolly was my mother). At once all the light and color seemed to be drained from my surroundings. I was blazingly angry with her, and wanted to shout, "No, I'm not! Why the hell should I be? And who are you to say so?" But of course I said nothing—to retaliate would have been considered insufferably rude —and walked on, pretending not to have heard, while my aunt proceeded to pass similar, though less unflattering remarks on the physical appearance of my sisters. I am not suggesting that my aunt's remark served as some sort of trigger for my disease, because I did not in fact become anorexic until three or four years later. Nor am I suggesting that one thoughtless remark can prompt a neurosis. What I am suggesting is that both my aunt's remark and her attitude stemmed from assumptions already prevalent within the family as to what was appropriate behavior. That this particular remark referred to my body illustrates in a pertinent and heightened form the treatment to which I and my sisters were subject as children.

Some further analysis of the incident is needed. The first thing that strikes me is that my aunt—an almost complete stranger as far as I was concerned—should have been there at all, within the family circle where no friend or neighbor was allowed, and thus in a privileged position to make personal remarks of the type which would not have been tolerated from any other quarter. Her remark was indicative not only of the close and exclusive family structure, but also of the petty rivalries and jealousies (in this case directed at my mother) within it. In the second place, it is clear that she had no idea what effect her remark would or could have had on me. She was following the family pattern of talking about children in their own presence in the third person instead of addressing them directly. This pattern implies that children have no thoughts or feelings of their own and are incapable of understanding the wider meanings of the simplest observations. But, as Morton Schatzman points out, this is far from the case:

> Certain words, especially if heard often and in childhood, may be encoded or transformed, stored, and later, in disguise, retrieved and re-experienced. I think everyone, some of the time, and some people nearly all the time, recurrently experience in and with their bodies literal meanings of certain oft-repeated speech they heard in childhood. That is, they translate words back into the same modality of bodily experience from which those who spoke the words derived them from within their own bodies.[2]

I consider this to be substantially true, and particularly true of my own childhood, although in this case there was scarcely any need for translation. The implications were that I had no physical characteristics of my own, but that in the same way as I "had" my father's nose, or my grandmother's eyes, I somehow inhabited a body which was not mine but a replica of my mother's, and over which, therefore, I had no control. So the remark was a climax to a series of similar remarks which I had previously received with only mild resentment or embarrassment. Schatzman again brings this point into focus: "Some, possibly all, people's bodies resonate to others' spoken words. . . . I think people called hypochondriacs are either talented at it (and unaware that they are) or have heard more 'physicalistic' speech in childhood than most people, or both."[3] In my childhood I certainly heard a great deal of "physicalistic" speech, such as "Isn't she sweet? I could eat her up," or "I'm not going to take that from him; it sticks in my throat." But most of it was concerned with family resemblances, which were sometimes not purely physical but characterological as well, and often to dead or very distant relatives. If we substitute the phrase "sufferers from a psychosomatic condition" for the word "hypochondriacs" in the Schatzman quotation, I think we have one of the ingredients in a recipe for anorexia nervosa. But Schatzman's point, like my own, is concerned with more than the "physicalistic" character of speech heard or overheard in childhood. To me, the third striking aspect of my aunt's remark is her ability or right to predict the future for me. This, too, was part of the family pattern. Just as I had been told repeatedly that I was destined to "do well," so then I was being told that I was destined to be "stout." It would seem that I had no choice in either matter, but whereas the former flattered me as well as frightened me, the latter insulted and enraged me.

"The family," says Minuchin, "is the matrix of identity."[4] True enough, and, despite the dissimilarities among families, the impressions taken from each matrix are likely to be of similar depth and importance. For an orphan or a child taken into care, the institution involved constitutes the family. For a child a hundred years ago, the family was likely to be an extended one, including aunts, uncles, cousins and grandparents as well as parents and siblings. Some time between then and now the unit commonly referred to as the family gradually shrank to a membership of two parents and their own children only—the nuclear family. Today an adolescent is probably as likely as not to belong to a family which is an uneasy mixture of the nuclear set-up and the institution known as serial marriage (marriage, divorce, remarriage). Of all these set-ups the most favorable breeding-ground for anorexia nervosa is the nuclear family—tight, self-enclosed and a world unto itself. Contrary to the popular image of the disturbed teenager, the anorexic is not typically a product of a "broken home," however unhappy that home may be. On the contrary, her home is a cohesive force, perhaps the only cohesive force she can experience in the generally fragmenting world of adolescence. Until recently it has tended to be a middle-class, if not an upper-class, home where the father prides himself on being able to provide well for his family, and the mother prides herself on being a good "homemaker" who runs the establishment with precise efficiency, giving careful consideration to the basic (i.e., material) needs of all the occupants. However, recent studies in comprehensive schools have shown that this picture is changing, and that anorexia nervosa is beginning to lose its class basis.[5] This is a subject to which I shall return, but for the moment I prefer to confine myself to the typical picture and to show where my own circumstances coincided with it or diverged from it.

My own family was at once strongly nuclear and part of what can only be called a clan. It was at first, through proximity, an extended family whose members were as strongly bound together as those who live within the nuclear structure. Later, when distance made such bonds unrealistic in everyday terms, the nuclear family became isolated, friendless, and therefore all the more determined to maintain the former sustaining links by whatever means were available. I was born, as were both my parents and their parents before them (and so on) on the Isle of Lewis in the Outer Hebrides. The Minch, which separates the island from the mainland of Scotland, is wider than the English Channel and much rougher. In winter the island is inevitably lashed by gales and snow-storms, boats don't sail, planes don't land, and communications with the outside world are often severed altogether. The result is a certain insularity which tends to be pervasive throughout the year, expressing itself in a fear and mistrust of strangers coupled with a fierce pride in the uniqueness of one's origins. In my childhood anyone who did not come from Lewis was scathingly described as a "forrinter." In extreme cases, the same description was applied to someone who came from a distant village. Because of the nature of the terrain—the land rocky and barren, the coastline highly indented—villages which appear to be close on the map can often be as far as 30 miles apart by winding road. In winter, these routes may become impassable, and so the village, like the island itself, may be cut off from outside communications. Life may be easier there today, but when I was a child few people had cars and buses were infrequent.

Cromore, the village where I was born, lies in the southern shore of Loch Erisort, looking across to a similar settlement on the northern side. At that time the houses were scattered and there was no village shop (the mobile shop called once a week), although there was a church and a school. My father was the village schoolmaster and I, like my sisters, Helen and Pat, was born in the schoolhouse, a solid, stone-built structure incorporating two large classrooms as well as the usual living quarters. It was built to last, and the vaulted classrooms now serve as tearooms for any tourists intrepid enough to reach them. When I revisited the place in 1974, I found it at once grim and beautiful, at once an irrelevance to my present life and a painfully inevitable part of what I was, what I am, and what I always shall be. The grimness was not only a matter of the appalling weather conditions, nor of the remoteness from all comforts and advantages of city life. It was also the grimness of Presbyterianism. In small communities with a strong religious nucleus there is always an element of censure—sometimes unspoken, sometimes whispered, more rarely shouted aloud and face-to-face—of those who are thought to have transgressed against the faith. I think my father must have suffered some of this, if only because he refused to have us children christened. I remember someone—the school cleaner, I think—telling me how dreadful this omission was, and how I recognized the mixture of shock and pity in her voice without being able to separate the two, or understand to whom they were being allocated and why. In other words, the place was a place where everyone knew everyone else's business.

Then, as now, people had nicknames as they do in Wales, and I have always suspected that this type of labeling has causes other than the lack of variety in local surnames. Jones-the-milk is all very well, but to be dubbed Murdo-foolish for the rest of your life is a different matter. I see the latter as symbolic of a process which has been described variously as "attribution" or "definition." In *Sanity, Madness, and the Family*, R. D. Laing and Aaron Esterson point up, with a clarity which I at once recognized and was astonished by, the importance of attributions within the family.[6] Briefly, an attribution is a description of one person given to her/him by another person and which she/he has difficulty in reconciling with her/his own self-image. The describer is usually an adult, the described a child. The attribution itself can either be total, e.g., "Claire is such a good girl," or partial, e.g., "Henry has a vicious streak." So far this is normal and to be expected, but if Claire is told often enough how good she is when she feels herself to be bad, or if Henry is constantly reminded of his vicious streak when he is aware of other, ignored qualities in himself, then both Claire and Henry are likely to become confused as to their own self-images.

Again, I think such feelings are commonplace, especially in adolescence, and that they can become diffused and thus manageable with a wider context than that of the rigidly nuclear family or the rigidly nuclear community, a context where attributions from outsiders can modify the original ones and lead the individual towards a reassessment of her/himself. But it is also clear that within tight-knit units attributions can become destructive: you are given your role and you must play it out, the same role for the rest of your life. This is what Thomas S. Szasz is implying when he writes about "definition": "In the animal kingdom, the rule is eat or be eaten; in the human kingdom, define or be defined."[7] He sees the struggle for definition as "veritably the struggle for life itself," and that to perceive oneself for oneself is a matter of life and death: "In short, he who first seizes the word imposes reality on the other: he who defines thus dominates and lives; and he who is defined is subjugated and may be killed."[8] Szasz is putting the position at its most extreme, but I recognize the truth in what he is saying and, apart from his implication that the definers are acting with conscious deliberation, I think he is right. On my last visit to Lewis I found myself repelled by the use of derogatory nicknames, and couldn't understand why I was reacting so violently. It was only on re-reading Szasz that I realized I had been touched on a sensitive spot—the struggle for individual identity—and that that spot was central to the problem of anorexia nervosa. It seemed to me that "eat or be eaten," a phrase with literal meaning in the animal kingdom and metaphorical in the human, is in anorexia re-interpreted and used through the symptoms of the disease with literal force.

But all this is hindsight: it is a series of thoughts and feelings which sprang from a visit on a painful occasion (my mother's funeral), and not from my childhood experience of childhood itself. Until recently I should have rejected the premise that my earliest years represented some sort of attack upon my individuality and insisted that, on the contrary, I was surrounded with kindness and loving care—as indeed I was. In fact, my childhood on Lewis can be described as a happy one. In many ways it could even be described as idyllic. In the conventional sense of the word, which conveys some sort of harmony with the natural world, it certainly was. There was the shore of the loch where we children could paddle, catch tiny sea-creatures (but always put them back in the water again) and collect all sorts of treasures. There was the school garden where the pupils learned to grow vegetables and I (being under school age) pottered around with them and after them, eager to help. There were the hens to be fed, their eggs to be collected. I was especially fond of my maternal grandparents' dog, Luath, an exquisitely patient collie with whom I would sit for hours, pretending or half-pretending that we could read one another's thoughts.

Inside our house there were stone floors, coal fires, oil lamps, but I don't remember ever feeling any sense of cold or discomfort, except when I got chilblains—a seasonal occurrence (and one which Dally cites, along with other circulatory disorders, as common among anorexics and perhaps indicative of a certain proneness). Nor can I remember any sense of restraint: the landscape belonged to me and I to it, and I was free to explore it and be nurtured by it in a subconscious Wordsworthian sort of way. Of course there must have been prohibitions and limits set, but I don't remember rebelling against any of them. I suppose I must have accepted that whatever my parents told me was good and right because I had no reason to think otherwise. They seemed to have a good relationship, agree about most things, and never, never row—at least, not in front of the children. When I was a teenager there were rows of a sort—mainly about the behavior of my sisters—but during the whole of my childhood I can only remember one. I don't know what it was about, but I know that it shocked me into the sort of terror that I didn't know I was capable of. And it is only fairly recently—probably since my mother's death—that I have been able to abandon the naive belief that such an apparently "perfect" relationship is indicative of a good marriage. Then, however, all was seemingly well.

In order to arrive at the truth behind the idyll, I must return to the matter of attributions. As I remember, the three adjectives applied to me most consistently throughout my early childhood were "clever," "good," and "healthy." Cleverness was by far the most important of the three. Just as Mr. Micawber can be characterized by his belief that something will turn up, so I was characterized by my cleverness. This would seem to imply a super-intelligence, but it was nothing of the sort. My cleverness consisted of verbal fluency and, more importantly, the concomitant skill of literacy. My father taught me to read at a very early age. According to him, I was able to read aloud to him passages from the *Stornoway Gazette* when I was three years old. This was generally considered to be brilliant, although it seems to me that it was as much

my father's achievement as my own, and probably perceived unconsciously by him as such.

Achievement, especially academic achievement, was what being
clever was all about. I was destined for great things—Oxford or
Cambridge, a string of letters after my name, a successful academic
career, and would no doubt end up being the first woman Prime
Minister. This sort of thing was impressed upon me, not only by my
parents, but by the whole network of the extended family. I should have
been pleased, I should have been flattered, and indeed I was. I thrived
on the praise and admiration, loved to show off, and secretly (or not so
secretly) thought myself superior to older children who had not yet
acquired my special skills. But even more secret, so secret that I could
scarcely even admit it to myself, was my sense of inadequacy. I read and
read, but increasingly, as I grew older, understood very little of what I
read. As far as I was concerned, reading was an automatic skill rather
than an indication of superior intelligence or understanding, and no
one but myself seemed to have noticed the difference, or even realized
that there was one. I have often wondered if this obsession with formal
education and the high value put on academic achievement is a
peculiarly Scottish thing, but it is clear from Bruch's studies that the
pressure to achieve—not necessarily but often academically—is an
important factor in the aetiology of anorexia nervosa. However, not all
girls under such pressure become anorexic. The distinguishing feature
in my case, as in those of Bruch's patients, was that I, the eldest, was the
only one in the family to be put under such pressure. I remember
discussing with my parents, years later when I was a student, some
recently published findings on the question of innate intelligence.
When I postulated that the environmentalists might have a case, they
were horrified that I *of all people* should express such a view, when it
had been clear to them from the start that I was different from the others
(my sisters). So they had decided, and so—in their terms—it turned
out. Apart from the youngest, all my sisters left school at sixteen or so
and got married shortly afterwards, whereas I went on to university. In
promoting my education and neglecting that of my sisters, my parents
proved themselves right. I had cleverness thrust upon me, and up to a
point I learned my lesson well: the most important thing in life was to

achieve. And not only that. It was equally important to outshine everyone else around me—in other words, to achieve at the expense of others. But by my late teens I had come to find this attitude repellent, and knew that I was never going to fulfill my parents' expectations.

Cleverness, like goodness and to a lesser extent, healthiness, was a feature of my status within the family—that of the eldest child. Bruch suggests that a significantly large proportion of anorexics are eldest or elder daughters.[9] And, in view of her theory that anorexics have a poor sense of their own size, weight and proportions in general, it may be interesting to examine more closely the status of the eldest child and more specifically the eldest daughter. The eldest child is a pioneer: it is she/he who first undertakes to make contact with the outside world, to go to school, and to make friends and thus set an example to younger children of what constitutes relationships outside the family. Although the parents are primarily responsible for establishing the norms in such relationships, the eldest child can find that it is she/he who bears most or all of the responsibility because the parents themselves are, like those of many anorexics, either relatively or completely isolated. Such a responsibility can prove onerous because a child who comes from an introverted home is likely to be introverted her/himself. If she/he does not or cannot succeed in forming friendships, she/he will become very lonely indeed, no longer belonging entirely to the family, and unable to belong in any real sense to the school and the peer groups within it. This must lead to some confusion in the perception of self for both girls and boys.

For girls the problem is compounded by the concept of mothering. The eldest daughter, even if she is not the eldest child, is much more likely to be asked by her mother to help in the care of younger children than is an eldest son. She will be asked to feed, change, pacify or amuse a baby brother or sister, and later to supervise journeys to and from school, or to take charge at home when both parents are out. Of course some boys may be asked to perform some or all of these tasks, but I think that (for historical rather than biological reasons) the task of substitute-mothering is more likely to devolve upon a girl than upon a boy who is in a similar position within the family. Such a girl is being asked to behave in many ways like an adult (mother) in that she is being asked to carry out the nurturing and supervisory procedures which properly belong to adulthood and, traditionally, to motherhood in particular. She is being asked to bear adult responsibilities but, because she is a child she is not, at the same time, granted any of the privileges of adulthood. Of course not: she is biologically unequipped for most of them. Again, there must be some confusion in the perception of self, but this time it relates directly to the perception of size. An adult is a woman, is a mother, is large and has power. A child is a girl, is small, incapable of motherhood and comparatively powerless. This dichotomy must surely give rise to resentment, however firmly repressed.

Popular mythology among mothers has it that the first child is always the most "difficult," and it is easy to see why this should be so. It is given to the first child, through no fault of its own, to disrupt what has been an exclusive, reciprocal relationship as no subsequent child has power to do. And I have been told that as a baby I conformed to this pattern, in contrast to my first sister who was "delicate" and my second sister who was "placid." As a baby I was fractious and for most of my childhood I was exuberant, passionate and hyperactive. But at the same time I was learning the lesson that such behavior is not acceptable to adults, to whom I presented a different personality. I stress the exuberance because most of the literature on anorexia nervosa stresses that anorexics tend to be "good" little girls. A good girl is, generally speaking, one who knows how to please adults and not to bother them too much. A good girl is obedient. A good girl helps her mother around the house and with the younger children, being especially good if she does so without being asked. Somehow or other I managed to learn these lessons, becoming anxious to please and to be praised for having pleased. My behavior was based partially on hypocrisy and partially on a fear of rejection. My especial goodness lay in my consideration for my parents ("Mummy is tired"; "Daddy has a migraine"), whose approval I was in fact terrified of forfeiting, and, perhaps as a consequence, in my attentiveness to my two younger sisters, of whom I was in fact bitterly jealous.

Most writers agree that childhood jealousy is common in the history of anorexics. Dally goes as far as to state that it indicates a bad prognosis for the disease, but I am glad to be able to report that although my jealousy continued into my adolescence, including the anorexic period, it did not deter my recovery, and that my sisters and I are now the best of friends. However, they have told me recently that, when I was about nine or ten, they thought me a bully because I would surreptitiously pinch them or pull their hair in order to keep them in line—that is, in order to make them behave as my parents would have wished them to. But outwardly I was all sweetness and patient understanding, continually being congratulated on my competence in the role of "little mother." As Menninger puts it, "Like all unacknowledged, unconscious aggression, excessive forbearance is self-destructive."[10] My aggressiveness towards the adults around me for putting me in such an invidious position was certainly unacknowledged and unconscious, and had my sisters not told me of my bullying tactics—which I had conveniently forgotten—it is likely that I should not be able to acknowledge it even now.

My healthiness, or sturdiness, as it was more commonly called, was another important aspect of my being the eldest child. I was two years old when my younger sister was born. She had a weak chest and needed a lot of attention, whereas I was robust and could be left to my own devices. I think I learned the lesson even then that the frail receive more love and attention than the healthy. I was desolated by the emotional separation from my mother, whom I thought the most wonderful person in the world. The story goes that, when she was nursing my sister, I said to her, "Put that thing in the pram and come play with me." I would follow her around the house, clinging on to her skirt, unwilling to let her out of my sight, and demanding to be fed with some small token such as an apple or a piece of bread. "A mother," says Elias Canetti, "is one who gives her own body to be eaten. She first nourishes the child in her womb and then gives it her milk. . . . "[11] What better revenge can there be on an unfaithful mother who gives her body to another than to reject her, and with her the principle of nourishment, in becoming anorexic? I could see my sister being nourished as I had been nourished, and I was demanding some sort of parity. But I don't think I got it. I had and have the distinct impression that my mother found me a nuisance. Perhaps that was one of the reasons which prompted my father to teach me to read, and so divert me from my inexorable pursuit of my mother.

As the mother of two sons myself, I now find my childhood reaction extreme, and am led to suspect that my separation anxiety originated some time before the birth of my sister. And because the anorexic girl's relationship with her mother is of prime importance, I think the suspicion is worth investigating, although what follows is necessarily conjectural. When my elder son was born and I was having difficulty in breast-feeding him, my mother sympathized with me and told me that, just after I was born, she had had an abscess on one of her breasts and found feeding me something of an ordeal. My own reaction at the time—a guilty feeling of my own inadequacy as both feeder and fed, mingled with a wish that she had not told me—indicates that this is an important piece of information. Feeding me must have been painful, and perhaps therefore an unpleasant emotional experience. It is possible that her attitude towards me could have been colored, even deter- mined, by her own suffering. And although this is conjecture, I feel it should be mentioned, if only because the primal mother-child relation- ship so highly emphasized in post-Freudian psychoanalytic literature has been largely ignored by those who have written about anorexia nervosa. Because I cannot rely on my conscious memory of my own earliest moments, I can do little to remedy this omission. But D. W. Winnicott may be helpful in this context in suggesting what sort of process might have been taking place. He describes a "good-enough mother," (i.e., a mother as good at being a mother as any of us can expect either to have or to be) as someone who "starts off with an almost complete adaptation to her infant's needs, and as time proceeds she adapts less and less completely, gradually according to the infant's grow- ing ability to deal with her failure."[12] In other words, being a "good- enough mother" depends largely on appropriateness of response.

In a striking image, Winnicott describes the mother's face as a mirror in which the baby perceives the image not only of her/himself, but of the whole world into which she/he has been born. When a mother's face does not reflect a meaningful world of which the baby is a part—as it seems to me the face of a woman in pain cannot—then what results is "a threat of chaos and the baby will organize withdrawal, or will not look except to perceive as a defense. A baby so treated will grow up puzzled about mirrors and what the mirror has to offer. If the mother's face is unresponsive, then the mirror is a thing to be looked at but not looked into."[13] In my own case, none of this is verifiable, and may seem far-fetched, but it is interesting to compare Winnicott's concepts of both good-enough mothering and the mirror-image with what Bruch has to say specifically about the mothering of anorexics. Emphasizing that the early histories of anorexics rarely give evidence of gross neglect, and that terms like "rejection" or "lack of proper love" are unhelpful, she concludes that "the details one learns are usually quite subtle; the important aspect is whether the response to the *child's needs was appropriate or was superimposed, according to what the mother felt he needed*, often mistakenly."[14] We are back with appropriateness of response: a mother who has difficulty in feeding her baby may persist, because she is anxious that the baby should be properly fed, in prolonging a painful experience beyond her own and the baby's endurance. If Winnicott's image of the mirror-image is a valid one and what the baby needs at a certain stage is a reflection of a meaningful world in which she/he has some place, we are also back with perception and self-perception. Mirrors, being the most readily available and most literal source of self-perception—a faculty which is always weak in anorexics—also play an important role in the symbology or symbolism of the disease.

To return from conjecture to fact: the nuclear family left Lewis in 1944 when I was five years old. I don't know why this decision was taken, especially as it doesn't seem to have been a well-planned one. My father had a teaching job in Leytonstone in East London, while my mother, my sisters and myself stayed with a series of relatives in both Scotland and England. Eventually we moved to Dorset where my father taught at the local grammar school. We lived for a year in a cottage attached to a remote farm—so remote that I have never been able to find it again. The conditions were primitive—no electricity or running water—and in a way it was a continuation of the life we had led on Lewis, except that the extended family had now shrunk to a nuclear and very isolated one. I sometimes think that this, the year of my sixth

birthday was the happiest of my life. It was also the year in which I
discovered both sex and death, so I must have learned something, in
spite of not going to school. Otherwise, it was a sort of limbo, and it
wasn't until we moved to a council house in Southall in the outer
suburbs of London that the shades of the prison-house began to close.
That phrase has never been a cliché to me, but an exact description of
what I experienced in 1946. When I read, later, Edwin Muir's
description in his *Autobiography* of his transition from Orkney to a
Glasgow glue-factory, I read also a description of my own (less
conscious, more childish) emotional state at the age of seven. Everything was noisy, dirty, speedy, and everywhere one was hemmed in by
houses, traffic, and people, people, people. I learned for the first time
what it was to be a stranger, an immigrant from primitive parts who
spoke with a funny accent and called things by their wrong names. I
soon learned to say as little as possible, meanwhile doing my best to
cultivate a London or "Cockney" accent, which my parents took great
pains both to prevent and to correct. They wanted me to talk "posh,"
and so, after a series of elocution lessons, I did.

It was then that I went to school for the first time, to a Roman
Catholic convent in Ealing, not because of my parents' religious beliefs
but because it was thought to be educationally superior to any of the
state-run schools in the locality. There I was always effortlessly top of
the class and almost totally friendless. That my parents were continually
making anti-Catholic remarks and pouring scorn on some of the more
devotional pronouncements of the nuns did not help matters. At school
the importance of baptism was stressed and, once, all those who had not
been baptized were asked to put up their hands. I was much too
frightened to do so, having been told that the unbaptized would be
consigned to hell, and—what was even worse—that in the eyes of God
we did not exist. It was less the fear of hell (which seemed a long time
away) than the fear of being a non-person which prompted me to ask my
parents if I could be baptized. I remember this fear quite distinctly as
that of being swallowed up into some great emptiness: the struggle for
individual identity, central to the phenomenon of anorexia nervosa, had
already begun, and already I was using the appropriate metaphor. My
request was dismissed with some amusement by my parents who added

that I should have more sense than to believe in all that mumbo-jumbo. I was eight years old at the time and completely confused by their attitude.

The early death of a sibling is an event which Dally cites as being common in the histories of anorexics, and a year or so later my baby sister died of bronchial pneumonia. She was, of course, unbaptized, and I was terrified at the thought of her burning in hell. One of the girls at school assured me that unbaptized infants were sent not to hell, but to limbo. However, being ignorant of either place, I didn't know whether the latter was better or worse. The nuns, trying to comfort me, said, "Think of her running around in heaven with all the little angels." In a desperate attempt to comfort my mother, I repeated this message to her. At once she burst into tears and hugging me for the first time in years (it seemed), cried, "If only I had their faith!" The loss of my sister was not entirely beyond my comprehension as it was beyond that of my other sisters. What I could not understand was the absence of consensus among adults as to what constituted death, and as to its meaning. My grief was exacerbated because I was now hopelessly confused, not knowing whom to believe, and needing to believe in someone or something. Soon afterwards I became openly rebellious at school and, after some final misdemeanor which I cannot recall but suspect to have been trivial, I was asked to leave.

I don't think those years were particularly happy ones for any of us. Whether or not my father was happy, I could not and cannot tell because that has always been difficult, but I suspect from his outbursts of temper and the frequency of his migraines that he was not. My mother was more obviously unhappy; she missed "home," as she never ceased to call Lewis, and her own family, and having someone to talk to in Gaelic, which was her first language but not my father's. The weekly arrival of the *Stornoway Gazette* was something to be looked forward to, and the paper (some of which was in Gaelic) read from cover to cover. Neither of my parents seemed to have any friends, and tended to talk disparagingly of neighbors or colleagues. Invitations were turned down on the grounds that "we would only have to ask them back." But my diaries for 1949-50 record visits to and from relatives, frequent correspondence with them, and frequent discussion of their affairs, especially their health. The family was still what mattered. After all, we were no ordinary family, but a clan: I was told by my mother always to hold my head up high, and remember that I was not only a MacLeod, but a double MacLeod—MacLeod being also her maiden name. How far all this was homesickness or a defensive strategy against (anticipated?) rejection by the surrounding community, or just sheer stubbornness, I now can't tell, but I knew even then that it had nothing to do with the world in which I was trying to live. What I have described is, I suppose, a typical picture of exile. Minuchin's description of an Italian immigrant family in America[15] parallels my picture, although it describes a more extreme situation. The anorexic in this family suffered from confusions similar to mine. Because of this, and because she, too, was rebellious, she is the only one of Minuchin's patients with whom I can identify.

For me by this time the Eleven-plus* was looming up, and in the conventional manner, I was promised a bike if I passed. It was impressed upon me how terribly important the "Scholarship" was, and how its result would determine the whole of my future life. Naturally, I was terrified. Because I was not attending school, my father undertook to coach me. I could do the English and the intelligence tests, but I was hopeless at mental arithmetic: for some reason my mind would go blank whenever I tried to visualize numbers instead of seeing them written down. This, I think now, was due less to innate innumeracy than to my father's teaching method. He would fire questions rapidly at me, sigh with impatience at my slowness, and urge me, "Come on, come on!" If I got a question wrong, which I did more often than not, he would repeat it in what seemed to me a contemptuous tone until I got it right. If I failed to do so, he would become exasperated and start shouting at me, telling me how stupid I was; whereupon I would dissolve into tears and rush out of the room. After all I was supposed to be clever. A diary entry of the period reads, "Daddy won't let me go out to play or listen to Children's Hour or read stories. All I'm allowed to do is study while the others do what they like. Not fair!" After this a short sentence has been

*A competitive qualifying examination taken by British schoolchildren at the age of 11 years, to determine selection for and placement in grammar school (British college preparatory school). It normally includes intelligence tests, and papers in arithmetic and English.

rubbed out (I wrote in pencil) so that there is a hole in the page. I suspect it was "I hate him," and that I couldn't actually bring myself to face such a sentiment. However, the word "Daddy" has been crossed out in ink and "my father" substituted. This, I suppose, was as far as I could allow myself to go. I certainly thought of him as a tryant: my diaries are full of complaints about unfair treatment, undeserved punishments (including the corporal variety) and arbitrary deprivations. Whether or not those complaints were justified is another matter; enough that at the time I felt they were.

I resented my mother too. It seemed to me that she should have taken my part, should somehow have defended me from my father. After I had fled the room, I could hear him say to her, "She's not even trying. I despair of her!" My mother would answer inaudibly, but it would be evident from my father's all-too-audible answering tirade that she had been gently remonstrating. Always, though, whether immediately or eventually, she would acquiesce, and I resented her acquiescence, not only because of its consequences for myself, but because I didn't understand why she, an adult, would not or could not stand up to him. Erikson sums up the situation well:

> The polarity adult-child is the first in the inventory of existential oppositions (male-female being the second) which makes man exploitable and induces him to exploit. The child's inborn proclivity for feeling powerless, deserted, ashamed and guilty in relation to those on whom he depends is systematically utilised for his training, often to the point of exploitation.[16]

The Eleven-plus, like all crises, threatened the pattern of family relationships, and all the family could do in order to maintain equilibrium was to ensure that each member remain entrenched in or return to his or her habitual role. And I should perhaps add that to this day I am practically innumerate.

But, much to my surprise, I passed the "Scholarship," got my bike, and went to grammar school. I was relieved, rather pleased with myself, and genuinely looking forward to entering a new, more grown-up phase of my life. But I was to be disappointed. There was something drab and uninspiring about the place: lessons were boring, teachers were boring, the other girls were boring. I had ceased to be good at the convent, and now I also ceased to be either healthy or clever. I was always being ill with minor ailments such as earache or tonsillitis, and often spent as much as three consecutive weeks away from school as a result. During those times I read a great deal—mostly books chosen for me by my father and which I thought more suitable for boys than for girls—Jack London, Rider Haggard, Talbot Baines Reed, Arthur Ransome. I fell behind in my schoolwork and in some classes, especially maths, I simply had no idea what was going on.

It was at this point, when I was twelve years old, that I took to reading junk books the way some people take to eating junk food. I read long-forgotten authors of books about girls' schools in Switzerland or Paris, as well as Angela Brazil, Noel Streatfield, Pamela Brown and, above all, Enid Blyton. How I envied the schoolgirls of St. Clare's or Malory Towers: they belonged to a safe, structured world where rules were rules, good was good, and bad was bad. And in spite of, or perhaps because of, this framework, they all seemed to have such fun, such carefree, girlish fun. My rebellion was only half-conciously directed at my father's choice of reading matter for me, although his disapproving and often angry comments made it clear that he took my behavior as a personal affront. I wanted to choose for myself, yes, but I also wanted to escape into a world of certainties, which I knew to be unreal while desperately wanting to believe that it might have some reality. I wanted to escape from being at home, from being at school and, quite consciously and openly, from being myself.

In a way I had given up. My life lacked the clarity, form and order of simple fiction, and I had no idea who, where or what I was or should be. But in another way some stubbornness was at work in me, some determination never to give up, and to cling in secret to whatever reality I could find for myself. With hindsight I can see that I was already predisposed, given the right circumstances, to become anorexic. But those circumstances did not arise until four years later, when I was not with my immediate family all the time, but away at boarding-school, the Malory Towers of my dreams.

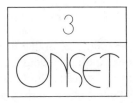

3

ONSET

In 1952 I received a county grant, enabling me to attend a girls' public school in the Home Counties. When my father suggested I apply, I was pleased and very excited at the prospect of going to boarding-school, which seemed to me to be an adventure, an escape from boredom. There were no examinations, only two short interviews, one with myself and one with my parents. One of the questions I was asked was, which historical figure did I admire most? Naming the first person I could think of, I answered St. Francis—because he could have chosen to live a life of luxury and ease, but had in fact followed the principles of Christ in giving away all he owned and living a life of poverty. It seemed like the right sort of thing to say. And it was righter than I knew, the school chapel being dedicated to St. Francis, of whom the headmistress was a particular devotee. I often wished later that I had named Trotsky instead, because his principles were more in accord with the way I felt about the place by the time I left, but at that time I had never even heard of him. My parents were asked about conditions at home. We lived in a three-bedroomed council house, one of the bedrooms being little more than a boxroom, and by this time there were seven of us in the family. Such overcrowded conditions, together with my father's low salary as a teacher, were probably as important factors as my own abilities in my being considered a suitable case for rescue.

Although I had wanted to go away and agreed to go away, when the time came I also felt that I was being pushed out of the nest, and that my parents were glad to be rid of me, in that there would be one fewer person to cater for. This was quite conscious on my part, but I was too proud to mention it to anyone or even to hint at any such thing. When I went home in the school holidays I had to sleep on the bed-settee in the "front room." My initial homesickness at school soon gave way to a dread of going home, home to a place where no one understood me, no one spoke the same language as I did, and no one showed the slightest interest in what I had been doing, thinking or feeling during my absence. My parents both showed interest in my academic work, and my mother some minimal interest in the personalities of my teachers or friends, but that was as far as it went. On the contrary, I was mocked within the family for my "posh" accent, and for what was considered to be my general childishness, especially as far as my sense of humor was concerned. I was also repeatedly chided for my exuberance, my feverish need to communicate with others, and to have friends outside the family circle. Home seemed drab, centered as it was around domestic duties and financial worries, and affording no opportunities for entertainment or emotional release. I was no longer a part of it, but this was something I could not, in my insecurity and because of my ingrained family loyalty, admit even to myself. Although I remember the hurt vividly, none of the sentiments I have just expressed appear in my diary: again, it was a matter of pride. And, besides, I had always been told that self-pity was despicable. So a process of self-deception began instead. All I could admit to was boredom, and the belief that school was more fun.

It seems strange at first that this should have been so. After all, I was more of an outsider there than at home, being out of my milieu and having none of the social graces or advantages of my fellow-pupils. Another "scholarship girl" was shamefully treated by the rest of us because of her (very slight) Cockney accent, her generally "non-U" turns of phrase, and her inability to deal with the simpler points of etiquette, whether at table or in the classroom. But I wasn't fool enough to give myself away. I listened and learned, watched and learned, and soon became adept at striking the first blow: if there was any teasing and tormenting going on (and there was plenty) I made sure that I was an active and not a passive participant. I lived by my wits. No doubt my verbal articulacy, being greater than that of my unfortunate companion, helped me in this form of self-defense, as it did in my ability to lie. I lied about everything: the size, style and location of my home; the possessions and social pursuits of my parents; and I even omitted to mention that I had sisters who went to "inferior" schools. The inevitable question, "What did you do in the hols?" would be greeted with a list of the films I had seen, and the dances and point-to-points I had been to, whereas in fact I was not allowed to go to the cinema (perhaps for financial reasons), had never been to a dance in my life, and didn't even know what a point-to-point was.* No one, as far as I know, disbelieved me. Because I was cunning enough to keep my lying within plausible bounds, I was able to deflect too-close questioning and avoid ostracism.

Lying about my family's social status came easily enough, but there was nothing I could do about the more visible signs of poverty. The chief of these, which I carried around with me, were my clothes. My grant covered the school fees only, and no provision was made for other necessities. The uniform, which we wore most of the time, was in my case obviously secondhand, being of an earlier model than the current one. I remember removing the name-tapes of the former wearers (who had left the school) with a savage feeling that these people had to be got rid of, otherwise they would possess me as a living person is possessed by a ghost. My shabby uniform soon became dirty and then dirtier, and once I was sent out of class to the matron by a teacher who complained of my general "filthiness." It had not occurred to her that my parents simply could not afford the dry-cleaning bills. My non-uniform clothes, which were worn in the evenings and at weekends, were also second-hand, bought in a secrecy which my mother insisted on, from a shop in Notting Hill. It was a perpetual anxiety with me that I should turn up at school wearing a dress that had been sold to that same shop by one of my fellow-pupils. The clothes were obviously not new. This fact could not be concealed any more than I could conceal, when a friend invited me to stay with her during the holidays in Yorkshire, that my parents couldn't afford the train fare. Neither could I conceal that although I wrote to my parents once a week (a school rule) they scarcely ever wrote

---

*A "point-to-point" is a form of steeplechasing.

to me, and failed to send me the necessary supplies of toothpaste, stockings, etc., so that I was always having to borrow from other girls (strictly against the rules) and getting into trouble as a result. For this I consciously blamed my parents: it seemed to me that instead of writing to me, as other parents wrote to their daughters, they had written me off.

My early years at the school were, then, a mixture of deception (on my part) and the fear of humiliation. The situation should have made me totally miserable, but at first it did not—at least, not in any overt or lasting fashion. Because there were compensations, I was able to transcend it. For the first time in my life I found myself surrounded by friends—friends whom I found interesting, and friends who appeared to find me interesting, bright and witty, despite my all-too-evident disadvantages. It was a gratifying experience to find myself liked and accepted by my peers to an extent that I had never expected. I became famous (or notorious) for my diary, which I kept up assiduously, and which was generally believed to be full of scandal of the sort the school authorities would not like to see appear in the newspapers. The scandal in question was, of course, the implication of female homosexuality. It seemed to us pupils that the authorities (teachers, but perhaps more especially matrons) were obsessed with preventing any such thing from occurring. Girls were not allowed to share wash-cubicles, hold hands or walk along arm-in-arm, and the washing of one another's hair—a fairly frequent happening—was severely punished. Close friendships with girls a few years older or younger than oneself were actively discouraged, and it seemed to us that to be seen in earnest conversation with a girl who belonged neither to one's own year or one's own house was tantamount to admitting that one was engaged in a lesbian liaison. How far any homosexuality in the physical sense went on I cannot say, mainly because I was rather naive about such matters, but rumors and counter-rumors abounded.

No, what we were interested in, at the age of thirteen or fourteen, were "pashes." (For the benefit of those who are unfamiliar with the word, a "pash" is a schoolgirl crush based largely on admiration, usually from afar, and a sub-sexual affection which is less in search of requitement than of acknowledgement, however minimal.) In fact, during my first two years at the school, this was almost the sole topic of conversation. Here again I was able to prove myself useful and to gain a little kudos: I could compose with what seemed to others an astonishing facility an ode or sonnet on behalf of some lovesick junior and addressed to some beefy, lacrosse-playing heroine in whom I myself had no emotional interest whatsoever. My services were much in demand, not only for sentimental verses, but for expressions of anger and rather cruel satire. Some of these efforts appear in my diaries of the period, along with detailed accounts of the amatory dispositions and sub-amatory activities of what seems to be the whole of the lower school. Anyone who has ever been to a similar school will know exactly what I mean. It is impossible to convey to an outsider in a few short words the hothouse emotional atmosphere of such an establishment, with its all-too-conscientiously suppressed sexuality, and the consequent hysteria, or just plain silliness. Anyway, it was an atmosphere in which I thrived. I delighted in the intrigue, in the drama, and in writing it all down. I had control over my material, which was life at school, and which was now my life to the exclusion of life at home. And I therefore had some control—just enough to keep me going—over myself.

For those first two years I was able to enjoy behaving childishly—a pleasure which I felt had been denied to me—and being relatively free from responsibility. In short, I could enjoy, rather belatedly, being a silly little girl. But puberty, or rather the onset of menstruation, changed all that. It should be noted at this point that the small number of boys who become anorexic (14 percent as compared to 86 percent girls of the patients studied by Bruch[1]) do so before they reach puberty and do not develop sexually until after they have recovered.[2] Girls, on the contrary, have almost invariably developed sexually before the onset of the disease. To me menstruation happened rather late, when I was nearly fifteen, and during term-time. It took me by complete surprise. That it should have done so was irrational, because I had "known" about menstruation since my grammar school days when girls used to boast about how they had just "started." I suppose the problem was that I had never been told about it officially—that is, by an adult—and so I had somehow blocked off the information, not connecting it with myself, with my own body.

With sex, or what are known as "the facts of life," it was different.

When my mother, in a state of total embarrassment, attempted to enlighten me, I had to help her out by telling her what I knew already. I was about ten or eleven at the time, but I had "known" since I was about six. The cottage we had rented in Dorset was attached to a farm, and the farmer had four sons, the youngest of whom was about my age. We were great friends, to the exclusion of my sisters whom we considered too young and soppy to take part in our adventurous games. Often, in the course of these, which involved a lot of wandering about among the surrounding woods and fields, we had occasion to urinate together (it would have taken too long to go home) and the opportunity to examine one another's bodies. At about this time my third sister was born. I had seen my mother pregnant, and had been told that she was carrying a baby inside her, a little brother or sister for us all. I also knew that somehow my parents had got together to produce this baby. When she was pronounced to be the image of my father, I suspected that something belonging to my father must have got inside my mother to the place where the baby was being carried. And so it was in the light of this suspicion that I examined my friend's body and my own. It was clear not only where the differences lay, but also that those differing parts were somehow complementary, intended to be fitted together. And I suspected that the long-term intention was to produce babies. The boy himself confirmed my suspicions, but although we were "in love," as boys and girls of that age so often are, we never attempted to put our theory into practice. It was tacitly assumed that such activities were for grown-ups only.

I'm sorry to disappoint orthodox Freudians, but I felt no penis envy, and didn't think myself to be maimed in any way. On the contrary, the differences between us seemed to strengthen the bond I had with the boy: when we grew up, *we* were going to get married and have babies. I'm also sorry to disappoint all those writers on anorexia nervosa who insist that the disease stems from a longstanding aversion to sexuality and childbirth. To me, it all seemed quite natural and even rather exciting—if a bit strange, but then no stranger than any other activities or preoccupations belonging to the grown-up world. And so I could help my mother out of her embarrassment. All she had to do was to confirm what I thought I knew already, and to give this knowledge an official seal of approval. "Now," she said with some relief, "you can tell the others when you think they're old enough to understand." This I did at once with a feeling of self-importance which blinded me to the now obvious fact that she was abrogating her responsibilities and allowing them to devolve, once more, upon her eldest daughter. Menstruation was not mentioned then, or at any other time, so it is hardly surprising, if rather bizarre, that I never made any conscious connection between it and normal sexual functioning.

Unlike the uninformed virgins described by Mara Selvini Palazzoli[3] (and who were, after all, Roman Catholics who traditionally place a high value upon virginity), I was horrified and disgusted by menstruation rather than by sexuality. I felt that some dreadful punishment had been visited upon me, punishment for a crime which I had never committed. But I think I knew unconsciously that the supposed crime was twofold: I was being punished for being female and for having grown up. At the same time I didn't *feel* female, in the sexual sense. Neither did I feel male, but rather neuter, as a child might feel itself to be neuter. And I certainly didn't feel grown-up. The crimes in question had been committed by my body, not by me. Such a split in self-perception is, I think, more likely to occur in girls than in boys at the time of puberty because the physiological changes which a boy undergoes are likely to be treated as marks of manhood, whereas what happens to a girl is more likely not to be mentioned, although in many ways the signs of her having reached puberty are more obviously visible. Ruth Benedict, writing of puberty ceremonies in various societies, sheds some light on this seemingly paradoxical cultural attitude.

> If cultural emphasis followed the physiological emphasis, girls' ceremonies would be more marked than boys'; but it is not so. The ceremonies emphasise a social fact: the adult prerogatives of men are more far-reaching in every culture than women's, and consequently . . . it is more common for societies to take note of this period in boys than in girls.[4]

The secrecy which, in my adolescence, surrounded menstruation was an indication of the inferior status of women in that society.

Perhaps I sensed something of this. What I felt consciously was anxiety, accompanied by shame, and at school the procedure for dealing with menstruation did nothing to diffuse either emotion. When a girl's period was due, she would sign a little red book hanging by string in the medicine cupboard, and the under-matron would discreetly place an unwieldy packet of sanitary towels in her underwear drawer. Tampons were not allowed, being considered unsuitable for unmarried girls. Old-fashioned or external sanitary towels, as anyone who has had the misfortune to make use of them will know, are dreadfully uncomfortable: they will not stay in place, they leak, and they chafe. Perhaps because my mother refused to send me a sanitary belt, saying that such things were unnecessary, I leaked and was chafed more than most. My underwear was invariably returned from the laundry with the comment, "v. badly stained." I felt myself to be a source of pollution, and grew to dread my period, especially as I never knew exactly when it was going to come. All these circumstances were barely mentionable, even among the girls themselves. I remember the humiliation of being told, in a shocked tone, that I had a big, red patch on the back of my summer dress. Everyone else seemed to have the thing under control. I had no idea whether anyone else felt as I did, suffered the same pre-menstrual depression or the same cramping pains. Needless to say, no one had ever told me about the pain, and I became convinced that something was wrong with me, but I was too embarrassed to confess as much to anyone.

If menstruation was hidden—in theory, at least—the bodily changes which accompany it were clearly observable and indeed the outward signs of its invisible presence. Perhaps it was for this reason that I hated them as much as I resented menstruation itself. But I think I resented them both for the same reason, that is, that something was happening to me, or rather to my body, which was completely outside of my own control. Given my background, as described in the previous chapter, it is not surprising that I should have felt particularly sensitive on this point. Being a late developer, I had been small and slim in comparison to most of my peers, and my appearance had been a large part of my character. It had implied a certain agility, both physical and mental, a general quickness or brightness. It also seemed to inspire a sort of motherly affection in others, so that I was more likely to get away with carelessness or naughtiness than were my more physically mature contemporaries.

Although I was still "tiny" (a word used by one of them at the time) by any normal standards, when I looked in the mirror, I saw someone who appeared to me to be "gross"—a favorite word with anorexics, as Minuchin shows. I had been a thing of firm, clear outlines; now I seemed to splay out in all directions and to have assumed a shape, thanks to undue accretions of flesh, which bore no relation to the person I believed to exist within it. "That," I told myself, "can't be me." Years later I was at first comforted to read that an adult man could express similar sentiments about himself: "When I consider others I can easily believe that their bodies express their personalities and that the two are inseparable. But it is impossible for me not to feel that my body is other than I, that I inhabit it like a house, and that my face is a mask which, with or without my consent, conceals my real nature from others."[5] But then it occurred to me that Auden's self-perception could have sprung partially from the necessity to conceal his homosexuality from his public. In my case there was no homosexuality—or heterosexuality, for that matter—to conceal, but I think there was a certain amount of gender confusion, nurtured by circumstances both at home and at school, which contributed to my sense of loss, the loss of self. I had lost so many selves before. Then I had rebelled, to the best of my ability, but this latest loss seemed insurmountable.

There were three factors which saved me from becoming anorexic at this dangerous juncture. The first and most obvious was the tactic of withdrawal into what little self I still possessed. Since there was nothing I could do about what was happening to my body, I decided—not altogether consciously—to ignore it and to interest myself in other, more spiritual matters. As a result of the "crisis of wholeness," which Erikson sees as marking the end of childhood, I was attempting to achieve a "sense of inner identity." As he explains, "where the resulting self-definition, for personal or collective reasons, becomes too difficult, *a sense of role confusion* results: the young person counterpoints rather than synthesises his sexual, ethnic, occupational and typological alternatives and is often driven to decide definitely and totally for one side or the other."[6] I decided, definitely and totally, to become a poet, and to devote my life to the pursuit of Literature. Science, history, politics, music—all these were insignificant compared to the magnificent calling I had chosen for myself. I read a great deal of poetry, especially the Romantics, learning long passages by heart, and found some solace there to lift me above the sordid realities of everyday life. More importantly, I began to write poetry myself, for myself, poetry which I showed to no one and kept hidden in an exercise book reserved explicitly for that purpose. This exercise book was, along with my diary, the only thing I could call my own. I still have it today, and I must admit that the "poems" indicate the desperation of a lonely adolescent rather than the promise of any talent.

The second factor was at first O-levels.* At the school the examinations were spread out over three separate sessions for each girl, so as to make the whole procedure as painless as possible, academic standards among pupils being generally low. For me, this system meant the weeding out of subjects which bored me, and the opportunity to concentrate and read around those which really interested me. The school had an excellent library, especially in the English section, and I would find myself immersed in the literary essays of T. S. Eliot, I. A. Richards, W. K. Wimsatt, Bradley or Dover Wilson, Maud Bodkin on archetypal patterns or Caroline Spurgeon on Shakespeare's imagery. At the same time I got some pleasure out of learning Kennedy's Latin Primer off by heart. In other words, I had something to aim for, an immediate goal. And these aims were ones I could share with others. So the third factor was friendship or, if there is such a word, colleagueship. It now became interesting and profitable to work with others, both in the classroom and in more leisurely periods of revision. Consequently, I began to develop different sorts of freindships, no longer based on silliness or naughtiness, but on joint and genuine attempts at co-operation and to understand not only the syllabus but ourselves and life in general. Superficially, I was coping, but I can see now that this period was a kind of moratorium.

---

*After five years of secondary education, academic students take the general certificate of education (ordinary or O-level) examination. This is a subject and not a certificate examination. After a further two or three years the brightest students take the advanced (or A-level) examination, usually only in two or three subjects.

It was not until the spring holidays before my summer and middle
O-levels that what can really be described as the onset of my anorexia
began. At home the family pattern had changed. We (or they, as I
would probably have said at the time) now lived in a detached, fairly
large house in a village in Berkshire; my father taught at a primary
school in a nearby village, and my mother had a job at the Harwell
Atomic Research Establishment. My sister Helen, now fourteen, was
attending the local grammar school, and during her holidays (which
were shorter than mine) she was still in contact with her friends, both
girls and boys. My sister Pat, aged thirteen, was in theory being educated
at home according to a syllabus devised by the Parents' National
Educational Union, and which worked on a postal basis in much the
same way as the Open University does today. This was quite legal
because my father was a teacher and therefore considered capable of
supervising her studies. In practice, she was taking my mother's place in
the home and spent most of her time fulfilling the role of unpaid
housekeeper. She also became anorexic later—a state from which she
was rescued by an early marriage at the age of sixteen. My two younger
sisters (who scarcely figure in this story) were at a local private school
run by nuns. I was more of an outsider than ever, but something in me
must still have wanted to belong to the family because I was still making
deliberate attempts to communicate with the other members. However,
all of these failed.

There was no real communication between me and my father, who
was also on holiday from school for much of this time. He commanded
and I obeyed, or, rather, pretended to. My task, apart from the usual
household chores, was to get on with the work for my three summer
O-levels and to get ahead by starting to work towards my A-levels—
English, Latin and Greek. Although I was still interested in English, I
found both Latin and Greek increasingly tedious: they were my father's
choice for me, not mine. I remember it was a beautiful spring and I
longed to travel, longed for company. My diary records the frequent
wish for "interesting people and interesting places." But whereas its
termtime pages are crammed with events and comments, the pages
belonging to these holidays are either blank or contain such comments
as "Forgot what did," or "Read, went for walk, did washing-up." In fact,

practically all I did was to go for solitary walks or pretend to read Virgil or Sophocles, whose two dead languages were now as meaningless to me as mental arithmetic, and as incapable of claiming my concentration. And yet I persevered. The following comment from Schatzman may perhaps show why:

> Parents and teachers, like writers of computer programmes, build certain sorts of information more deeply and irreversibly than others into their systems (children); in the idiom of computer engineers they hard-programme them. What is hard-programmed cannot easily be changed; to do so would mean a drastic re-ordering of the system.[7]

I did not know then what I was to find out later—that I myself was capable of a drastic re-ordering of the system. Then I resembled in some small way the unfortunate Daniel Paul Schreber, a German judge whose case was analyzed by both Freud and Schatzman, and whose father's "view of a good parent-child relationship was like the relationship between a hypnotist and a subject in his power: a child who experiences a glance, a word, a gesture of the parent as a command resembles a person in a trance."[8] I was in just such a trance, going through the motions of doing what I was told, but without being able to do so in reality. By the end of the holidays I was only capable of reading such publications as *Woman's Own* or *Valentine* without my mind wandering. At the time I ascribed my inability to an acute sense of boredom (which, in part, it was), but I can see now that it was also a form of rebellion, this time an unconscious one. I simply didn't know how to rebel openly. As Erich Fromm suggests,

> Perhaps the most important factor which leads to a weakening of self-assertion is an authoritarian atmosphere in family and society, where self-assertion is equated with disobedience, attack, sin. For all irrational and exploitative forms of authority, self-assertion—the pursuit by another of his own goals—is the arch sin because it is a threat to the power of the authority; the person subject to it is indoctrinated to believe that the aims of the authority are also his, and that obedience offers the optimal chance for fulfilling oneself.[9]

I think my father's authority was irrational because he expected me to have no other interests outside my schoolwork. And I think I believed, or tried to believe, him when he repeatedly told me that the restrictions he placed upon me were for my own good.

In all this, including the boredom, there is nothing new in the annals of adolescence. My relationship with my father had not changed, although I should have welcomed some change, since the days of my early childhood: it is difficult for most parents to admit that their children are growing up and therefore in need of a more flexible parental attitude. And my relationship with my mother was not much better. During the week I hardly saw her. What had happened, because his holidays coincided with mine, was that my father had become my mother as well as my father, in the sense that it was he and not she who was always at home.

He spent a lot of time in his study engaged in the writing of some mysterious work. But his labors were interrupted by frequent migraines, which sometimes lasted as long as three days, during which he would lie in darkness on the floor of his room, eat nothing, and demand silence from the rest of us. When he was up and about, he also spent some time in the kitchen, having become what was then called a "health-food fanatic." He used wholemeal flour to make bread, scones, pies and cakes, concocted elaborate salads and dosed himself with vitamins. I saw nothing strange in his behavior, but it is evident from the literature that the families of anorexics often include a member who either suffers from a psychosomatic complaint or shows an obsessive interest in food and its health-giving properties. The person concerned is, generally speaking, the mother, but, given the role reversal which I experienced during the school holidays, it seems reasonable to point to my father's behavior as a possible contributory factor to my becoming anorexic. It certainly contributed in a more direct manner in that most of the food we ate had a high carbohydrate content and, although I was unaware of it at the time, I put on a lot of weight. All I can remember is that I didn't much like the food, but I ate obediently and probably out of fear of giving offense.

Every evening my mother would come home from work, tired, and it seemed to me that she was only interested in her job or, more specifically, the personal affairs of her colleagues. But during the weekends I did my best to claim her attention, following her about from room to room as I had done as a small child, and chattering endlessly about life, literature and the events of the previous school-term. She didn't stop me talking, but neither did she reply or make any comment on what I had to say. She seemed to be suffering me in silence, as she suffered everyone and everything else. I was desperately seeking some sort of reassurance, some sort of comeback from someone, but it soon became plain that I was not going to get it from her. She gave me the impression that I was an utter bore (which I probably was) and something of a freak as well. I was not like my sisters.

Helen and Pat both wore fashionable clothes—circular skirts, padded bras, clinging sweaters—and make-up. I wore jeans or the demure dresses approved of by the school authorities. To me, my sisters looked flashy and cheap. To them, no doubt, I looked laughably dowdy. Their clothes and their make-up were directed towards one end—the acquisition of boyfriends. Meetings were held in secret—the boy with the bus fare or the motor-bike waiting at the end of the lane—and elaborate lies told as a cover-up until my parents got wise to what was going on. They argued endlessly about it. "You tell her." "No, you tell her." "You're her mother." "You're the one who's getting so worked up about it." My father would rage and storm, not so much at my mother as to her, and against Helen and Pat in their absence, but in the end neither of them would say anything to either of my sisters.

As a mother of adolescents myself, I now find this combination of intolerance and inaction extraordinary, although it would seem to confirm Selvini Palazzoli's point that the parents in anorexics' families are both unwilling to assume leadership. The real, open rows, my sisters have since told me, came later and when I was away from home. Meanwhile an atmosphere of tension and suppressed resentment prevailed. In the circumstances I should have been the good daughter, studious and uninterested in boyfriends. But not at all. It was made clear to me by my mother, sometimes backed up by my sisters, that as far as the opposite sex was concerned, I didn't stand a chance. Whatever sexual rivalry was going on was among the three of them, and I was excluded, being too obvious a failure to present any sort of threat. It seemed to me that I had become what my parents had wanted me to be, and I was getting no thanks from either of them for my efforts. However, I now see that there could have been less concurrence between them on this matter than I had supposed, and so I was a disappointment to both of them.

I didn't know any boys, except those I met through my sisters, and they seemed to me to be vain, impolite and almost totally inarticulate. The plain fact of the matter, snobbish though it may sound, was that they were both unintelligent and ill-educated in comparison to myself, belonging as they did to a different social class from the one into which I had been co-opted at school. But I was so anxious to please or, more accurately, to avoid the stigma of being abnormal, that I did manage to find myself a boyfriend. His attitude towards me was one of dumb, doglike devotion, which I found tiresome, but in the circumstances he seemed better than no boyfriend at all. "What an unusual boy he must be," my mother remarked, "if he has the sense to see beneath the exterior to the person inside." Needless to say, I didn't find this remark helpful, however well-intentioned it might have been. I refused to see the boy again, and spent hours anxiously examining my exterior instead. It seemed to me that it was wanting in every detail, but the objective facts were that I was five feet two and a half, weighed 117 pounds, and had my fair share of acne. Both physically and emotionally I felt myself to be younger than (inferior to) my two younger sisters. The competition was too strong, and so I opted out. At the same time I didn't want to be like them. If they were feminine, then I was not. But, because I felt even further away from being masculine, I was forced to amend this self-assessment and tell myself that I was *not yet* feminine. And I think it was at this stage that I made the unconscious decision, later to manifest itself in physiological terms, to postpone sexuality until I felt myself ready to cope with it.

On the conscious level I was at first glad to get back to school for the summer term. There at least there was no talk of boyfriends; there at least one or two people valued me; and there, at the very least, I knew what I was up against. But there, too, I found that things had changed. Most of the girls in my year, though not necessarily my friends, were leaving school at the end of the term. Their talk had turned to the world beyond O-levels: finishing schools in Switzerland, modeling or secretarial courses, steady romances with the sons of their parents' friends, or the heady excitement of the debutante season. I could no longer ignore the differences between myself and my companions, and I could no longer lie about those differences, but kept quiet instead, withdrawing further into myself. I didn't envy them their individual futures, which seemed dull or trivial to me, but I did envy the fact they had futures at all, whereas I had none, or, at least, not one to which I could look forward with any confidence. They also had a present. They were now the self-confident, responsible young ladies they had been trained to be by both the school and their own families. They organized events for charity, gave concerts, formed clubs, and were generally beginning to become part of the administration. They seemed to enjoy both cooperating with teachers and wielding power over juniors. At the same time they could become excited about house matches or school matches and take part in such events with earnest aggressiveness. All this I found despicable. I had no interest in charitable works, or in clubs devoted to flower-arranging, debating futile motions or even poetry-reading, seeing such activities as being designed to fill out the time of future ladies of leisure. I was anti-authoritarian, and had no intention of becoming authoritarian myself. And I loathed all sport to the point of finding its ethics repellent.

My dilemma points up a basic dichotomy in the educational aims of the school. On the one hand we were encouraged to be young ladies, polite, modest, and considerate towards others, especially those who belonged to the lower social orders. Religion was important here, inculcating as it did the traditions of service and good works. It was, of course, the perfect training for a housewife, even if the house in question were a stately home. On the other hand, the school aped the traditions of the boys' public schools, encouraging competitiveness and aggressiveness within a rigidly hierarchical structure which depended on eccentric but unbreakable rules. In neither area was there room for the development of the individual through creative work. Such an omission was not peculiar to this particular school, I realize, nor is it peculiar to schools of its particular type. As Jules Henry points out in discussing American schools,

> It stands to reason that were young people truly creative the culture would
> fall apart, for originality is by definition different from what is given, and what
> is given is the culture itself. From the endless, pathetic "creative hours" of
> kindergarten to the more abstruse problems in sociology and anthropology,
> the function of education is to prevent the truly creative intellect from
> getting out of hand.[10]

I am not suggesting that I was a "truly creative intellect"—merely that I
was denied the opportunity to find out whether I could achieve any
such position, and this was an omission I felt very keenly.

I became a loner, but I had to work at it. Solitude was an eccentricity
the school was at pains to discourage, and its absence gave rise to a sort
of panic in me which served to reinforce my sense of loss of self. For
those who are unfamiliar with such establishments, a description of a
typical school weekday follows. 7:00 a.m.: rise from a bed in an open
dormitory shared with five or six other girls; 7:30: breakfast, followed by
bedmaking; 8:30: early morning lacrosse practice or running round the
lake; 9:00: chapel; 9:20: three periods of lessons or prep; 11:20: break for
buns and milk; 11:40: two periods of lessons or prep; 1:00: lunch; 1:40
approximately: a house meeting in which each of thirty-six girls had to
inform the housemistress of her activities for the afternoon, and other
house business was discussed; 2:00: lacrosse (tennis, cricket, running)
or, if the weather was bad, country dancing, or, with luck, a shampoo;
3:20: wash and change into non-uniform clothes; 3:45: tea; 4:00: four
periods of lessons or prep; 6:40: house prayers; 7:00: supper; 8:00 or 8:30,
depending on age: half an hour to be spent in chitchat with the
housemistress in her room; 8:30 or 9:00: bathtime followed by bedtime.

So, in theory, someone of my age had half an hour of free time,
although it was in fact impossible to find any place where one could be
alone. Saturdays followed the same pattern, except that evenings were
free. On Sundays there were two full-length chapel services, walks
outside the school grounds, an hour of silent reading, and a similar
period for letter-writing and mending clothes. The rest of the time was
free, but of course there was still no privacy. I was forcibly reminded of
these circumstances when I read Minuchin's description of an
anorexic's family in which there were "no closed doors"[11] and where the
anorexic girl felt that all her actions, even her thoughts, were ob-

served by others, and therefore as much their property as her own.

Two of the prime needs of adolescence, I have found both from my own experience and that of my children, are those for privacy and the opportunity to participate in a subculture. When adolescence is enforced or prolonged, as it tends to be in closed institutions, these needs become all the greater. For me, privacy was a rare commodity, and I had cut myself off from the subculture which had once sustained me—only to find that there was nowhere else to go. Here is another of the paradoxes of anorexia nervosa: I must, in my unconscious, have wanted to grow up, but at the same time I was determined not to, because the models of potential adulthood with which I was presented were either repugnant or impossible to attain. Liam Hudson suggests that "it may be that a single system of values embraces the individual's perceptions of academic institutions; his perception of himself and his demonstrable behaviour," and goes on to say that,

> the oppositions between authority and freedom, self-expression and self-control, and masculinity and femininity are among the basic conflicts around which an individual's life develops and that they cover his responses to a wide range of logically unrelated issues . . . they represent some of the earliest developmental crises through which each individual in this particular culture passes: the impact of parental authority; the demand for self-control, first physical, later verbal; and the establishment of a satisfactory sexual identity. [12]

It can and will be seen that the particular academic institution in which I was incarcerated, together with the pressures of my home life, was not conducive to the resolution of any such developmental crises. Powerlessness, too, corrupts, as Rollo May has put it, adding a maxim from Edgar Z. Friedenberg: "All weakness corrupts and impotence corrupts absolutely."[13] May connects impotence with the loss of a sense of significance, and the corruption he has in mind is the sort that erupts in acts of apparently senseless and arbitrary violence, especially in large urban populations. I find his thesis correct in general, but should like to add that the corruption which amounts to violence is likely to be suppressed in someone who has been trained to be a good little girl and can, as one of his own case histories demonstrates, express itself in other, less overt, terms.

As I became more withdrawn, so I became more secretive and more cunning in finding ways of being alone. I soon learned to differentiate between the occasions on which I would not be missed, like chapel, and those on which my absence would be obvious, like team games where positions were allotted in advance. By now most of the other girls found me extremely odd, but they were easily cowed by my outbursts of sarcasm. Teachers found me irresponsible and anti-social, and for this I had to suffer. At school there was an iniquitous system known as House Order, according to which all the girls in one house were graded from one to, say, thirty-six, the criterion being the individual's worth to the community. Usually the grading took place within one year only, the Upper Fifth, for example, being considered inherently superior to the Lower Fifth. But in my case an exception was made, and girls from the year below mine were moved above me in House Order, as well as being made monitors who had special privileges. One had just won her school colors, and the other had raised a lot of money for the Endowment Fund by collecting empty jam jars. Meanwhile, I had written a play which was performed within the house and was enjoyed by all concerned in it. Nevertheless, I was told that I had "contributed nothing constructive" to the life of either the house or the school. Perhaps this sounds like a trivial complaint, but within that small, inescapable context I felt my demotion to be a deep, undeserved disgrace. It was public humiliation––the last thing I needed.

In discussing identity formation at adolescence, Erikson posits that it is partly "dependent on the process by which a society (often through subsocieties) identifies the young individual, recognising him as someone who had to become the way he is and who, being the way he is, is taken for granted."[14] It seems clear to me that no such thing was happening to me, either at home or at school, the former structure being too self-absorbed to take me into account and the latter too rigid. When the process described by Erikson is successful, "the community in turn feels 'recognised' by the individual who cares to ask for recognition; it can, by the same token, feel deeply—and vengefully—

rejected by the individual who does not seem to care." My play was my last bid for recognition and the last occasion on which I was prepared to recognize the community in reciprocity. From then on, the school had as much reason as I did to feel rejected, and if they perceived my rejection as vengeful, they were right.

I had felt this incident to be the last straw, but it wasn't—quite. As a misfit, I was not entirely alone. I had one friend from another house who felt the same way as I did about the school and the whole process we were being put through. She, too, was a "scholarship girl" and we prided ourselves on being the two most intelligent girls in the place. This may or may not have been true, but we were the most critical and non-conformist. When she announced she was leaving at the end of the term, I felt this to be the final betrayal, although I could not blame her, even then. Her parents had had the sense to realize how unhappy she was, and had made alternative arrangements. It had not occurred to me that alternative arrangements could or would have been made, but, the more I thought about it, the more leaving the school seemed like the most sensible thing to do. Accordingly, I wrote to my parents and, having pretended for years that I was relatively happy at school, I now confessed that I was utterly miserable, and begged them to take me away. For once, a letter came back promptly—from my father. I was being utterly foolish; my duty was to stay on, do A-levels, and go on to Oxford or Cambridge (which took an extra term); the local grammar school was not good enough to fulfill this latter purpose and if I went there, I would only be throwing my education away; and, besides, did I not realize that, in the face of difficulties, one should never give up, but struggle on and thus establish a superior strength of character? Happiness (or unhappiness) was not mentioned, and I assumed that it was of subsidiary importance.

I could have written back to explain that my life was a daily humiliation and an unrelieved imprisonment, but I felt sure that they would neither care nor understand and, again, pride deterred me. I could have run away, but I had no money and, even if I had been able to borrow it, I should still have been too frightened because I had nowhere to run to. If I ran home, I should only have been sent straight back, in even deeper disgrace. And I couldn't think of anywhere else.

The sensible thing would have been to turn to someone, some sympathetic teacher, perhaps. But I trusted no one. I suppose now that I could have freaked out and started smashing the place up, getting myself expelled as a result. But the thought of actual violence never occurred to me, although there was plenty within. I did the only thing I could: I became anorexic.

There was nothing conscious or deliberate about my decision, if indeed it can be called a decision at all. Even my rejection of food was not embarked upon deliberately. All I knew was that my life was intolerable and that the only way not to be destroyed by it, or by "them" as I called the adult, authoritative world, was to reject them and everything they stood for. I had to make some sort of last-ditch stand. When teachers, matrons, the housemistress and finally the headmistress all started to show some concern and more disapproval at my uncooperative (anorexic) behavior, I refused to answer their questions, or even to talk to them at all, and during the course of their homilies I merely stared out of the window or smiled to myself in a superior, scornful sort of way. I would shrink away in instant horror from the hand that placed itself on my arm or shoulder in an embarrassed and half-hearted attempt at communication. All this time I said nothing to anyone of what I truly felt. Of course I can see now how infuriating this behavior must have been. But it was only the beginning.

4
EUPHORIA

I stated in the last chapter that, in becoming anorexic, I did the only thing I could. I should now clarify that statement by rephrasing it: I adopted the only strategy open to me in order to preserve any sort of identity, however precarious, and in order to believe in myself as an individual being, separate from both the family and the school. Anorexia nervosa is fundamentally about an identity crisis. And because this phrase has been much abused and misunderstood, it may be useful at this point to refer back to Erikson, to whom we owe it in the first place. He describes the progress of an individual human life, necessarily rooted in its social context, as a series of such crises, the goal of each being a further step towards wholeness, towards a complete identity. It seems to me indisputable that, in our culture, adolescence constitutes just such a crisis—perhaps for many people the major one—but because it is one with which we are all familiar, I do not intend to delineate it in detail. Instead I shall confine myself to what I find directly relevant to anorexia in Erikson's writings on adolescence.

Distinguishing between personal identity, "the perception of self-sameness and continuity of one's existence in time and space and the perception of the fact that others recognise one's sameness and continuity,"[1] and ego identity, he defines the latter as,

> more than the mere *fact* of existence; it is as it were the ego *quality* of this existence. Ego identity, then, in its subjective aspect, is the awareness of the fact that there is a selfsameness and continuity to the ego's synthesising

methods, the *style of one's individuality*, and that this style coincides with the sameness and continuity of one's *meaning for significant others* in the immediate community.[2]

It should be clear from the previous chapters that although I still had some sense of personal identity when I became anorexic, I simply did not have the opportunity or know-how to form an Eriksonian ego identity. The distinction is important because it leads to yet another paradox inherent in the anorexic predicament. Without some sense of personal identity, the willful manoeuvres of the anorexic would not be possible: either suicide or madness might prove a better "choice" of solution to the individual's problems. But in the presence of a strong ego identity such manoeuvres would not be necessary. What I am trying to say is that the anorexic has sufficient sense of identity to know that identity is something to be fought for—by whatever means. Elsewhere, Erikson describes adolescence as "the age of the final establishment of a dominant ego identity" and the point at which the future "becomes part of the conscious life plan."[3] He concludes that,

> The process of identity formation seems to support an individual's ego identity as long as he can preserve a certain element of deliberate tentativeness of autonomous choice. The individual must be able to convince himself that the next step is up to him and, no matter where he is staying or going, he always has the choice of leaving or turning in the opposite direction if he chooses to do so.[4]

I find the phrase "deliberate tentativeness" a particularly sensitive one to apply to the identity problems of adolescence, in that it allows the individual the right to fail and to try again, to prove that she/he is capable of autonomous action. If anorexia is about identity in general, it is also specifically and most importantly about autonomy.

Autonomy is important to everyone, but I think it is fair to say that it is of particular importance in adolescence. It is then that a crisis of autonomy can be most nearly identified with a crisis of identity, and can be seen in many an act of teenage rebellion. The question to be raised in this context is, why does the anorexic "choose" that particular form of rebellion, make that particular bid for autonomy? My insight into my own motivations in "choosing" anorexia began when I read this statement: "Addiction, obesity, starvation (anorexia nervosa) are political problems, not psychiatric; each condenses and expresses a contest between the individual and some other person or persons in his environment over the control of the individual's body."[5] This was the most cogent view of anorexia nervosa I had ever come across. All I had heard or read before was the usual superficial assumption that the disease was a matter of slimming which had somehow or other (no one ever said how) got out of hand. But Szasz's observation struck me with the force of revelation. And he goes on to ask some similarly pertinent questions: "To whom does a person's body belong? Does it belong to his parents, as it did, to a very large extent, when he was a child? Or to the state? Or to the sovereign? Or to God? Or, finally, to himself?"[6] I recognized those questions as pertaining to myself at the time I became anorexic. What was happening to my body—not only the changes brought about by puberty, but the fact that the clothes it wore and the food it consumed were chosen for it by someone else—was a metaphor for what was happening to me as a whole person.

I think I seized upon that metaphor in order to turn it to my own advantage. I had nothing; I was nothing. More positively, I was being given what I did not want (which amounted to being given nothing) and being classified as what I was not (which amounted to being classified as nothing). My only weapon in my bid for autonomy was to go on strike. Withdrawal of labor, in the literal sense, would have been impractical and, more importantly, would have caused further destruction to my self-esteem in that without work (schoolwork) I should have had and have been less than the nothing I already felt myself to have and to be. So I "chose" a form of passive resistance. Just as the worker's ultimate weapon in his negotiation with management is his labor and the threat of its withdrawal, so my body was my ultimate and, to me, only, weapon in my bid for autonomy. It was the only thing I owned, the only thing which could not be taken away from me. My motivations were not as clear-cut as those of any contemporary workforce, but there is no doubt in my mind that I was going on strike in the only way I knew how to, and that in this sense Szasz is right to describe anorexia nervosa as a political problem.

Even so, this assertion raises as many questions as it answers. I have, in part, answered the question, "Why the body?" and I hope to be able to answer it more fully by using a different approach. Polanyi suggests that,

> the relationship between mind and body has the same logical structure as the relationship between clues and the image to which they are pointing. I believe that the paradoxes of the mind-body relationship can be traced to this logical structure and their solution to be found in the light of this interpretation.[7]

This is a statement, in more general terms, of the conclusion reached by Freud in his treatment of hysterics: he was able to relate a specific physiological symptom, such as facial neuralgia, to a specific and painful psychic event, such as a bitter remark received years earlier by the patient as a slap in the face.[8] In this case, a drama involving the relationship between mind and body was being played out. The process, known as "hysterical conversion," is described by Fairbairn as a defensive technique "designed to prevent the conscious emergence of emotional conflicts involving object-relations. Its essential and distinctive feature is *the substitution of a bodily state for a personal problem*; and this substitution enables the personal problem as such to be removed."[9] The parallel with the anorexic process is clear, and the reasons for such a substitution in both cases are probably similar. Both hysterics and anorexics have almost invariably been middle-class women or girls. Those who posit a purely biological basis for this phenomenon are ignoring the class or political element. It is not a view which includes the recognition that educated, underemployed women are singularly lacking in personal autonomy, and so prone to a frustration which is not necessarily or primarily sexual. Yet it is one with which both hysterics and anorexics seem to have concurred overtly, while rebelling, often despite themselves, by the only means available to them.

Although I believe that hysteria, as classically defined, can provide only a part of the answer to the problem of anorexia nervosa, it is a starting-point and, in the light of Szasz's observation that "hysterical conversion is best regarded as a process of translation,"[10] I propose to translate the history of my own symptoms back into the language in which they were intended to be expressed. My decision to adopt this method is not an arbitrary one. Neither does it imply that my approach to anorexia nervosa is based on orthodox Freudian psychoanalysis. Jung was of the opinion that Freud's greatest achievement probably "consisted in taking neurotic patients seriously and entering into their peculiar individual psychology. He had the courage to let the case material speak for itself."[11] In my capacity as my own analyst I feel that the least I can do for my patient, and my readers, is precisely to "let the case material speak for itself." But at the same time I should like to show that the speaking is by no means straightforward speech. In dealing with anorexia nervosa we are dealing with metaphor—sometimes a startlingly apt form of metaphor. It is for this reason, following on from Freud and Szasz, that I propose to treat my patient as a text. But I take my immediate clue from the American critic, Norman Holland: "unity is to the text as identity is to a person; or you could say, identity is the unity I find in a person when I look at him as if he were a text."[12] Given what has already been said about identity, it is unlikely that we shall find in the anorexic a unity of text. It is my belief that anorexic speech (or, more literally, behavior) consists of two quite separate and often contradictory texts, and that it is only by studying them both, in order to fit them together and so come up with an amended text, that we can understand what is going on inside the anorexic herself.

When I gradually began to eat less and less it was with no thought of slimming in the normally accepted sense of the term. I know that many girls who become anorexic set out with this express intention, and may even be able to persuade themselves that this is the sole cause (whole truth) of their subsequent condition. I know, too, that the stomach, on receiving less and less food, will shrink and gradually require less and less food at any one time. If this were indeed the whole truth about anorexia nervosa, it would be a straightforward medical problem, and therefore comparatively simple to resolve. But it is not.

The first question to be asked of the slimming thesis is, why do people, especially young girls, want to become slim? The answer is, in order to look good or, more bluntly, in order to become (more) sexually attractive; slimness in our culture being an essential ingredient of sexual attractiveness. In other words, to slim is to take a rational decision with a conscious aim in view. When that aim has been reached, the slimmer will abandon or moderate her strict dietary habits and try to maintain what she considers to be her ideal body weight. My case, like so many of those studied in the literature, does not bear out these facts. What, for instance, would have been the point of my striving towards sexual attractiveness? I was in an all-female establishment, and, even when I was out of it, lived in an almost exclusively female world. As far as I was concerned, men and boys constituted a separate species, with whom I had nothing in common, and the last thing I wanted to do (had I given the matter any thought) was to arouse their interest, which I feared might be predatory. I had no conscious aim in view. If I had, I should also have had the sense to know when I had achieved it, and therefore when to start eating normally again. Although the slimmer and the anorexic are both to some extent governed by anxiety, there is an important difference between them. Slimming is a conscious process; anorexia nervosa (being more than non-eating) a largely unconscious one—at least at the outset. In observing the behavior of the slimmer and the anorexic, we may read the same text, "I want to lose weight." But the sub-texts differ. Whereas the slimmer's reads, "I want to be a sexually attractive woman," the anorexic's reads, "I want to shed the burden of womanhood." Slimming is basically a matter of vanity. Anorexia is much more a matter of pride.

Loss of weight has meanings other than slimness. The most obvious is thinness: anorexics are not slim, but thin, often to the point of appearing almost completely fleshless. An anorexic may tell her friends or parents, "I'd like to be slim," and, if pressed for a reason, may reply along the lines of, "So that I can wear nice clothes, date good-looking boys, and generally have a good time." These conventionally acceptable statements constitute the apparent text of her behavior. But the sub-text texts reads somewhat differently: "I want to be *thin* because I don't like flesh." Flesh, female flesh, is to the anorexic an imposition from outside and, in extreme cases, an imposition of something swollen, polluted, dirty. Mara Selvini Palazzoli quotes a dream related by one of these latter cases: "On my way home from the convent I stopped outside the hospital. A woman who had just given birth was being lifted off a stretcher. I was horrified by her swollen and distended stomach. I heard them say that she had been brought to hospital because her belly was still full of urine."[13] My reaction to female flesh was neither as extreme nor as ignorant as that, and it was only my own, not that of other women, which caused me to feel revulsion. I have described how I looked in the mirror and, seeing myself "in the flesh," did not recognize myself. My horrified, "That can't be me" soon became a determined "That won't be me." But I had no idea how to implement my refusal and, when I began not to eat it was out of apathy and depression, out of a hopelessness concerning myself (including my body), rather than according to a definite plan.

The inescapable fact is that I didn't want to be a woman, although I was unaware of this at the time. What I did know was that I didn't want to grow up, and my diary records that I confessed as much—when pressed—to my housemistress. To me, the adult world was not a place where the individual could act freely and achieve growth, both in the acceptance of responsibility and in the likelihood of success. To me, it was just another place where I would be pushed around, perhaps even more violently than I had been before. Jung suggests that "something in us wishes to remain a child; to be unconscious or at most conscious only of the ego; to reject everything foreign, or at least subject it to our will; to do nothing, or, in any case, to indulge our own craving for pleasure or power."[14] Such a wish, which presumably applies to both men and women, seems as impossible of fulfillment as my determination, "That won't be me." And Jung's phrase "something in us" implies that the wish constitutes only a small element in the psyche—one that is not difficult for a sensible, mature person to reject, once she/he has recognized how unrealistic it is. But for me, it was difficult to reject and, far from being a minor psychic element, became a major obsession. The miracle of anorexia is that this wish can be fulfilled: one does not have to grow up; one does not have to become a woman, even in the biological sense; one can reject all foreign substances, for which food is a metaphor, and subject them to one's will. This is power indeed. Once the process is under way, it all seems easy: the only attribute required is an initial and stupendous effort of will. My non-eating started from positions of helplessness, of hopelessness, of a barely deniable adulthood and an even less deniable womanhood. By the time I had become fully anorexic, all these unwanted or unwelcome positions had been reversed.

At school we were weighed regularly—at the beginning, middle and end of each term—and it had been customary for me to record my weight in my diary on all these occasions. At the beginning of the O-level summer term I weighed 115 pounds and, if I was pleased at having lost two pounds, I certainly didn't say so. The omission is meaningless: I could well have been delighted, although I can't remember whether I had actually begun to think consciously about weight in terms of pounds at this time. By half-term I weighed 107 pounds, and I suspect it was only then that I became weight-conscious in the literal sense.

During the first half of the term, my diary scarcely mentions food, apart from the occasional comment on the revolting nature of some too-frequently presented dish. This in itself is odd because in previous terms I had often (though not regularly) described meals in detail. As anyone who has ever been confined to a closed institution will know, meals are events: they are the landmarks in each repetitive day, often providing the only elements of novelty or surprise in an otherwise predictable routine. I think I didn't mention food in my diary during this period because I didn't want to mention my own eating-habits. Maybe I was worried that someone else would read my diary, but if so this worry could only have been a slight one: I was much too careful to afford anyone the opportunity to snoop. It is more likely that the elements of secrecy and self-deception involved in my behavior were already so strong that what I was actually doing couldn't be described in words at all, least of all in the incriminating written word. If I had used words, I should have had to think more carefully about what I was doing. I was, so to speak, keeping the secret even from myself. Having recently re-read my own, I have come to the conclusion that diaries furnish the perfect vehicle for self-deception and self-enhancement, provided that, in later years, the reader/writer is incapable of reading between the lines or unable to remember what has been left unsaid. I can remember exactly what I was doing and, out of context, my behavior seems so harmless that the need for secrecy appears quite mysterious. I was refusing second helpings of food, asking unfailingly for small helpings, and skipping optional meals like tea or Sunday breakfast. It was what was going on in my mind that had to be kept secret, on pain of interference, on pain of ridicule, on pain of punishment and, inevitably, on pain of self-understanding. It was this: the less I eat, the more I am getting away with.

O-levels began ten days after the half-term weighing session, and if anyone noticed the drop in my weight, I suppose they attributed it to anxiety over the forthcoming examinations. In fact I wasn't particularly anxious, although my diary is full of the usual teenage moans and groans about the impossibility of absorbing any more information, and the exams themselves are described as "foul," "really foul," or, at best, "not very nice." I knew very well that I was going to pass them all. And my new-found confidence was not unconnected with my weight loss. I had already achieved something; I had already proved to myself that I was capable of independent achievement. This discovery made it all the more important to me to maintain my behavior and to maintain it in secret. I told myself that my intention was maintenance of the *status quo*, but this was at best a half-truth. The truth was that I didn't know how to effect such an aim, and if I found myself eating any more than the minimum—that is, enough for me to remain undetected by the authorities—I considered myself guilty of backsliding, and had to punish myself by eating even less the next day or at the next meal.

After O-levels there was still a month of term to go, a month in which I had ample time to devote myself to my obsession. Although I read a great deal, and wrote a great deal, meal-times were still what kept me going. But whereas before meal-times had implied some sort of positive interest in eating, their purpose now was the active avoidance of eating, the opportunity to prove to myself that I was still achieving, still winning. I would now ask for very small helpings, eat perhaps a mouthful, and then smear the rest of the food all over the plate, hiding the residue underneath an upturned fork. My diary records such incidents as, "Had to eat another roll at breakfast, much to my disgust," or "M. insisted that I eat another piece of toast, so I walked out in disgust." (It should be noted that the word "disgust" is being used in both cases with literal force.) I was becoming more upfront, and not just as far as food was concerned. Instead of withdrawing and being generally anti-social, as I had been, I began to argue with people —teachers and pupils alike—and to disrupt other people's activities for the sake of disruption. Having lost weight, I was beginning to "throw my weight around." My diary is full of diatribes against the childishness, laziness, conceit or inefficiency of others. I had emerged from apathy into active aggression, and my housemistress's report for the term includes the advice, "Sheila must learn to curb her natural exuberance." I went home for the summer holidays weighing 104 pounds. And at the beginning of the following term I wrote in huge letters on the front of my rough book (regularly inspected by the housemistress), "Exuberance is beauty."

So my resolve had not weakened during the holidays. I had spent some time on a camping/cycling holiday with my family in the West country. I didn't enjoy it, but for me there was one advantage: there were no regular meals, and so no one noticed how much or how little anyone else ate. We shopped in village stores as we went along, and my diary lists items of food bought rather than consumed. At the beginning of the holidays I spent a week with a schoolfriend in London, and towards the end another week with another friend in Bedford. During those two periods my diary makes no mention of food, and I assume I must have eaten more or less normally. During the time I spent at home I seem to have eaten nothing but apples and, if I am to be believed, an inordinate number of them. Only the entry for August 15 reveals some alleviation of my anorexic anxieties in a reaction which is, at the same time, typically anorexic: "O-level results came today. Have passed them all, thank goodness. Cooked huge meal to celebrate. Ate masses." Because there are no expressions of regret afterwards, I assume I felt entitled to some sort of reward. But for the last two weeks of the holidays I was continually feeling "sick" and "shaky," and went back to school, weighing 99 pounds.

This time—at last—someone must have noticed what was happening to me. The entry for a week later reads: "Had to go to Hospice. Dr. ordered no games, extra rest, milk, butter, cream!! Nothing wrong with me at all really! The housemistress even presented me with a glass of milk at lunch. Ugh! . . . Had to have butter at supper, which I refused to eat. I don't see why I should, if I feel all right. . . . Matron said I had to go to bed early for a fortnight. This place is so depressing!" The battle was on, and was to continue for another year. The school authorities decided that my diet was to be strictly supervised, and that I should be weighed every week. At first it was easy enough to evade supervision, and my weight remained stable for several weeks. But at the end of October, a diary entry reads: "Was weighed and have gained 2 lbs—am now 101 lbs! Went to see Dr. and was on Gym for 1st time this term. Had to play games too, and felt dead. I wish I were. I hate this place!" I felt I was beginning to lose the battle, and the diary for the remainder of the term is full of expressions of hatred for the school, interspersed with the repeated and heartfelt question, "Why can't they leave me alone?" By the time I went home for Christmas, I had gained another pound.

Whether or not the school communicated any concern for my health to my parents I don't know. I don't remember that the question was ever discussed at home. My diary for the holidays is, as usual, almost blank, but contains several references to having overeaten and then feeling sick, which served me right. Nevertheless, I went back to school having lost four pounds. I now weighed 98 pounds, the lowest figure I had yet attained. The general reaction was, "Anyone who can actually lose weight over Christmas must be ill." But the doctor could find nothing physically wrong with me, and the notion of seeking psychiatric help doesn't seem to have arisen. I was put back on the diet designed to "build me up." This time the supervision was stricter, and it became more difficult for me to pass my butter ration on to someone else, to pour Ovaltine down the sink behind the matron's back, or to dispose of extra food by means of the lavatory. But I had also become more cunning. I think it was about this time (I can't tell exactly because my diary makes no reference at any point to the practice) that I discovered purging. How this happened, I don't remember, but I suppose it was a case of a desperate situation demanding a desperate remedy. I soon found out that if I swigged a mouthful or two of the laxative *cascara sagrada* from the medicine cupboard, I could get rid of the obnoxious feeling of weight and fullness which had been forced on me. The sinking stomach pains which heralded this loss were always welcome to me, and afterwards I would feel triumphantly clean.

It must have bewildered the matron, who watched practically every mouthful I ate, that by the end of term I had lost another two pounds. The diary entries for the Easter holidays are even sparser than usual, but when I went back to school I had lost yet another two pounds. This time the diary entry reads: "Weighing. 93 lbs. It's awful. I must go up." But of course I didn't think it was awful at all, and was in fact extremely pleased with myself. I pretended to be as puzzled as everyone else was about the nature of my "mysterious illness."

Meanwhile I continued the strategy I had been following for the previous two terms: feigning compliance with the authorities and responding cooperatively to their apparent concern, while continuing to eat minimally and to purge in secret. By the end of the summer term I weighed 85 pounds.

Two facts emerge immediately from this resumé. The first is that I felt my battle to be with authority, whether in the form of teachers, matrons, parents, or even nature itself. The second is that, up until this point, I was winning. It seems to me that anorexia nervosa acts as a metaphor for all the problems of adolescence. But instead of meeting each problem separately and assessing it for what it is, the anorexic thinks she has a master-plan, designed to solve them all at one stroke. She is convinced that it works; it can't fail. It is like a dream come true. It is euphoria.

When I first came across Szasz's dictum, "Mental illness is a self-enhancing deception, self-promoting strategy,"[15] I considered it to be a harsh judgment on a suffering fellow-creature. But when I substituted "anorexia nervosa" for "mental illness" I could see the truth in what Szasz was saying, and realize at the same time that his judgment was not so harsh. After all, if the self is felt to be nothing, any strategy adopted to enhance or promote it, desperate though it may be, is a step towards what most of us would consider to be health, and an action necessary for survival. The anorexic's skinny body proclaims, "I have won; I am someone now."

But thinness, as opposed to slimness, also carries connotations of weightlessness and emptiness. The sub-text to be read in that skinny body is, "I am weightless/worthless; I am empty/nobody. This is what my behavior is all about." The strategy works by means of paradox, a paradox which has ultimately to be resolved through some sort of fusion between the apparent text and the sub-text. But in the first, euphoric phase of the disease, only the apparent text is granted recognition by the anorexic.

I have said that the anorexic starts from a position of helplessness and hopelessness, and I have tried to demonstrate that this was so in my case. As my weight decreased, so did my helplessness. Anorexia provided me with the illusion that I was in control, not only of my body and my own status within the community, but of that community itself and, finally, of the biological processes which others around me were powerless to influence. In short, I became convinced of my own omnipotence. The conviction started from my body and the discovery that no one could prevent me—if I were determined enough—from treating it as I wished. I had discovered an area of my life over which others had no control. And although the sub-text of my increasing thinness (which I chose to ignore) read, "I am doing this because I feel so helpless that not even my own body belongs to me," the apparent text read to me, and increasingly to others, "My body is my own and I can do what I like with it." At first I was exhilarated to be able to make such a statement. I had considered my body to be lumpy, untidy, anomalous and entirely unsuited to the person within. My behavior had accordingly been unstructured: I was lazy, untidy, uncommunicative, forgetful and generally inefficient. But when I managed to convert my body into something trim and neat, my personality changed too. I became lively, hard-working, and so well-organized that I found inefficiency in others deplorable.

My diary, in my pre-anorexic days, often refers to a "weight of depression" which I felt myself to be carrying around. Once I became anorexic, that weight vanished with my flesh. My step lightened, I was full of energetic high spirits, and during the summer term I even became keen on playing tennis, which I would practice with the assiduousness I had formerly devoted to the piano. At night I would often get up and go for long walks in the school grounds, especially when the moon was full and I felt particularly restless, enjoying the silence and solitude of the woods. I don't remember ever being afraid, and I would boast of my nocturnal activities to a few close friends, who were duly impressed. As far as the physical aspect of this sort of behavior is concerned, the apparent text read, "My body is strong and healthy, super-healthy, despite your insistence that I am ill." But, as Bruch has pointed out, anorexics tend to deny fatigue, and my diary is full of complaints such as, "felt dead tired." So the sub-text of my behavior could be interpreted as, "I feel weak and tired, but I'm damned if I'm going to admit it, because that would only prove you right." Far from making any such admission, I became more and more fanatically energetic as the disease progressed.

If my body was now trim and neat, redeemed from the excrescences of flesh, it was also clean. When I reached 90 pounds or so, my periods stopped. I mentioned this to no one for two practical reasons: one was that I loathed swimming, and if I pretended that I was still menstruating, signing the little red book every four weeks, I should be able to evade an unpleasant experience for at least one week out of four; the other was that I feared further reprisals might be taken against me. It was easy enough to deposit the unused sanitary towels in the school dustbins during my nocturnal wanderings. But the main reason for my silence was that secrecy and deception had by then become second nature to me. I didn't want my periods to start again. That I had managed to stop them was a major achievement on my part. Instead of growing up, I had, as it were, grown down, and thus reversed a natural biological process. I was no longer a woman. I was what I wanted to be: a girl. I was what I felt unconsciously I had never had a chance to be: a little girl.

I rejected womanhood, not because I preferred manhood, but because I preferred girlhood. At the time my idea of manhood was personified as someone who had to work hard at a job he hated in order to support not only himself, but other people whose very existence he resented; someone who was forever having to make difficult decisions and take frightening initiatives, both of which ended in frustration; and someone who might be called upon to fight in wars (National Service was then still in operation) and kill people. This was not an attractive proposition, but my idea of womanhood was hardly preferable.

In her attempt to ascertain why anorexia nervosa is a girls' rather than a boys' disease, Selvini Palazzoli emphasizes the manner in which the adolescent girl "is exposed to lewd looks, subjected to menstruation, about to be penetrated in sexual embraces, to be invaded by the foetus, to be suckled by a child, etc."[16] I find this emphasis generally correct in that it describes what the anorexic girl believes to lie in store for her as a woman: a passive role, a position of helplessness, a loss of self. It is what she has experienced already, but with the addition of responsibility, pain, and bodily suffering exemplified in the bearing of children and the shedding of blood.

When I was anorexic I had only dim feelings of resentment as to how my body was destined to be used, and the thought of anything as positive and specific as penetration never entered my mind. Incredible as it may seem, I never thought about sex at all, and didn't even masturbate: starvation reduces libido. However, I now see my very sexlessness as a flight from sexuality, and mainly *my own* sexuality. I think I was afraid that, once I recognized it, it too might get out of control—just like my body in general. On the conscious level, sexuality was to me only one of the responsibilities of adulthood: as far the sexual act itself was concerned, I simply didn't want to know, as a child who is exposed to sexual information at an age when she/he feels incapable of absorbing it will not want to know. And I use the word "responsibilities" rather than "pleasures" because whereas no one had ever discussed with me the possible pleasures of sexuality, the responsibilities of adulthood had been habitually stressed, both at home and at school. With the weight of my flesh, I had also shed the weight of responsibility.

It seemed to me obvious at the time that to be a child was safer and easier than to be adult and that, specifically, to be a girl was safer and easier than to be a woman. As far as I was concerned there were two types of women, the true type and the failed type. The true type, as personified by my own and other mothers, was destined to bear child after child, some of whom could miscarry, some of whom could die, and all of whom were a perpetual source of worry and expense. This true type, having found her man, was forced to accept that biology was indeed destiny. But I couldn't accept any such thing. The failed type of woman, as personified by most of the teachers at school, had been unable to find a man. All the same, they were no freer, no happier, than the true type. It was generally assumed among the pupils that our teachers, being women, would have preferred to be fully sexual, childbearing beings. But instead they were "dried-up old spinsters," miserable biological failures. At that stage in my life I couldn't take any kind of failure, and so this latter model of womanhood was as unacceptable to me as the former. I think too that because I had postponed rather than rejected sexuality, the latter model was even less acceptable. But, for the time being, the rejection of womanhood had to be complete.

When I looked in the mirror and told myself, first, "that can't be me," and later, "that won't be me," what I was seeing was a woman. In my rejection of the image I saw I was making a statement, the apparent text of which read, "I don't want to look like (be) that." And I think I was right to make the equation between "look like" and "be" because a woman *is* what she looks like. That she is so is essentially an untruth, but it is at the same time a socially undeniable fact, even today, although it was probably a more widespread one 20 odd years ago. It is also a fact which should be given careful consideration in the attempt to determine why it is that girls rather than boys tend to become anorexic. When a man looks in the mirror, he can tell himself, "You may be an ugly old devil, but you're brilliant/successful/virile." When a woman looks in the mirror, she sees the totality of her being: because of the social brainwashing to which she has been subjected, the mirror seems to tell her more than it can tell a man. And so my sub-text read, in part, "I can't cope with this; I'm not going to be any good at it." The flight from womanhood was linked with the flight from failure, the fear of which had practically been bred into me.

Thus far the sub-text had a certain logic, but fear (or, rather, anxiety) can lead to panic, and the second part could have been expressed as, "I don't want to be a woman because I would rather be myself." On the face of it, this was an illogical statement, but by becoming anorexic I refuted logic. When I eventually weighed under 80 pounds and looked at myself in the mirror (which, in common with other anorexics, I did a great deal) I saw someone beautiful: I saw myself. No matter what anyone else thought or said, I was beautiful: I was myself. The clearer the outline of my skeleton became, the more I felt my true self to be emerging, like a nude statue being gradually hewn from some amorphous block of stone. This is the distortion of perception referred to by Bruch, but I must add that in my case I see it less as a longstanding perceptual difficulty than as a consequence of my general state of confusion as to my self-image. To see my starved self as beautiful was to dissipate a large part of this confusion: I was, literally and metaphorically, in perfect shape.

The distortion of perception extended itself to areas other than my body. Having disposed alike of unwanted flesh and unwanted menstruation, I had become pure and clean, and therefore superior to those around me. I was so superior that I considered myself to be virtually beyond criticism. The intellectual form of superiority was the one most accessible to me both at home and at school. At home it was a simple matter for me to parade my learning in front of my sisters, stressing my more advanced academic achievements at every possible opportunity, and remaining quite oblivious to their assessment of me as an insufferable little prig. My attitude to my mother was similar: I would feign amazement at her ignorance of the intricacies of the Punic Wars, while at the same time snobbishly correcting her pronunciation or her misapprehensions of social niceties.

With my father I had more difficulty: all I could do with him was to argue about literature, citing my teachers' opinions as being more up-to-date and therefore more valid than his own. At school I worked hard, spending most of my time in the library. Anything less than a straight A disappointed me, and even when I had clearly gained the best grade in the class—a slightly alleviating factor—I still told myself that it wasn't good enough. My reading was not confined strictly to the syllabus, and my book-list for the period shows that I was prepared to read around it. As I remember, I was even readier to advance in class the theories of, for instance, F. L. Lucas on the decline of the Romantic ideal, or E. M. Y. Tillyard on poetry direct and oblique, while suspecting that none of the other girls (or perhaps even the teachers) had read the books in question. People were impressed—maybe too easily. I didn't fully understand everything I read, and although the apparent text of my behavior was, "Look at me—how learned and knowledgeable I am," the sub-text was something more like, "I'm trying frantically hard to learn and to understand, despite my stupidity. Give me some credit. Tell me I'm not so stupid." The book-list also shows that I read Virginia Woolf, Aldous Huxley, Samuel Butler, Maxim Gorki, Henry James, Samuel Beckett, and so on. I have always been a quick reader and my capacity, not to say my voracity, was generally admired. I felt good. But perhaps I was as oblivious at school as I was at home to the sneers or the impatience of others. At the euphoric level of the disease, the anorexic perceives only what she wants (needs) to perceive. Anything else would only threaten her hard-won sense of unique achievement.

From this stage I proceeded to a more general sense of superiority, which can only be described as moral. At school I would follow certain rules in an ostentatious manner (while breaking others in secret) and become severe, even morally censorious, towards those who lapsed from my hypocritically high standards. Most of these rules, I should point out, were petty, automatic ones relating to punctuality or tidiness and can generally be described as "going by the book." At home I "rationalized" (the word used in my diary) the kitchen cupboards, according to a system in which items most frequently used were most accessible, and vice versa. I cleared out the forgotten corners which exist in every family home, sending old clothes to jumble sales, and asking boy scouts to collect useless piles of old newspapers and magazines. I tried to take over the kitchen, but in this I was thwarted by my father who had his own ideas about food, and who would keep interfering and making a mess, whereas I preferred to clear away and wash up as I went along. Whenever I did succeed in preparing a family meal, I insisted that everyone eat whatever was placed on her/his plate. Serving large helpings, I ate nothing myself and my abstinence was only another proof of my moral superiority. The apparent text of my behavior, openly declared, read, "I'm superhuman. I don't need food," and the sub-text, admitted only to myself and ignored as far as possible, read, "I'm starving." Similarly, the apparent text of my obsessive orderliness read, "Form and order make for efficiency, and efficiency makes for a well-structured, meaningful life," while the sub-text read, "Unless I impose some form and order on life, I shall lose control, chaos will ensue, and life will become meaningless." My twin obsessions were food and order.

It is at this point that the analogy between anorexia nervosa and hysteria, which Freud saw as separate from and possibly opposed to the obsessional neuroses, seems to break down, along with Dally's separation of the two as different forms of the disease. Both terms may be outmoded by now, but I think that in view of what I have already said about gender confusion and gender avoidance in my own case, they may not be entirely unhelpful. In Freudian terms, I had taken upon myself the typically female neurosis of hysteria along with the typically male one of obsessiveness. Nevertheless, it is Adler rather than Freud who sums up for me what was happening at this stage of the disease. Delineating his theory of retreat into illness as a means of obtaining power, he wrote, "Every neurosis must be understood as an attempt to free oneself from a feeling of inferiority in order to gain a feeling of superiority."[17] Although I denied being ill and scorned to make the demands for attention usually employed by invalids or malingerers, there is no doubt that I was by this time making a bid for power. The sense of superiority I gained was essentially related to control and, eventually, to the triumph of the will. The apparent text of superiority read, "I am in control. I can influence events and people. I am all-powerful. My will is supreme." But the sub-text, willfully suppressed, read, "I'm terrified that I have no control over events, over other people, over myself. Everything is arbitrary and therefore meaningless."

It amazes me now how little of this sub-text was legible to those around me. I suspect that my parents simply took my word and my active behavior as proofs of my essential health, and that my non-eating was something I would grow out of and could therefore be ignored. The possibility that I might starve myself to death was never raised: instead I was scolded for looking like a scarecrow, and my mother told me that she was ashamed to be seen with me. At school I was told by the matron that I would die if I continued to lose weight. I didn't believe her: my sense of superiority had extended itself to include a conviction of my own immortality. But I humored her, agreeing that she and I should cooperate in order to save my life. Thus I deceived her into thinking that she had scared me, and that I would take the necessary steps to ward off fatality. Outwardly it must have seemed that I had overcome my emotional difficulties and, apart from the mysterious phenomenon of my continuing thinness, had become a bright, helpful, well-adjusted member of the school. I told myself that I was happy, that I was free at last. In a way I was happy: I had achieved something, I was winning for the first time in my life, and I had a strong sense of myself as a differentiated individual. But the combined sub-text of my behavior, which I shall deal with in the next chapter, shows that this was far from being the whole truth about my psychic state.

As for being free—to be in thrall to a ruling obsession is hardly to exist in a state of freedom. I thought I was doing what I, and I alone, wanted to do, but my pursuit of academic superiority shows that I was still striving to be the person my parents wanted me to be. And my excessively tidy and authoritarian behavior shows that I was striving to be the person the school wanted me to be. Up to a certain point I was succeeding in both roles, driven as I was towards success by anxiety and the fear of failure. In reality, I was back where I had started—in a position of helplessness and hopelessness—but with one important exception. I now had something I could call my own: my disease, my unique neurosis, which I perceived as my thinness. The connection with neurosis was not unconscious, nor yet fully conscious in the sense that I could have expressed it verbally, but it was, in being unique, all-pervasive. Perhaps this may help to explain the determination of the anorexic to go on starving herself: without anorexia, I should have been nothing. I know that I had no intention of stopping the procedure, whatever anyone said or did to influence me. I was determined never to give in.

5
DEPRESSION

The euphoric effects of fasting have often been described by mystics, hunger strikers and others who have spiritual or political reasons for their actions. Perhaps their attitude can be summed up in a nice little phrase from one of Dally's patients: "The pleasures of eating are fleeting, but the pleasures of fasting are lasting."[1] It is those who suffer from chronic malnutrition, caused by a poverty to which they can see no end, who are more likely to give evidence of the depressive effects of starvation. In countries (or social classes) where such poverty is endemic, anorexia nervosa is unknown; it is a disease of affluence. But even those of us who have never been anorexic and live in the affluent Western world must know, perhaps through some isolated experience of our own or others', that non-eating leads to fatigue and thence to depression. Both the anorexic and the mystic are impervious to this simple chain of events. I myself have no inclinations towards mysticism whatsoever: I see it as a conscious attempt to transcend the exigencies of the material world, including poverty, in the interest or pursuit of some higher mode of consciousness. And in my experience, this sort of transcendence is not involved in anorexia nervosa, where the material world has to be grappled with and controlled, rather than dismissed as an ultimate unreality. The mystic surrenders his will to some being or idea which he considers superior to himself, whereas the anorexic strengthens her individual will against the impingements of an apparently inescapable reality.

Nevertheless, there are similarities between the two: both are empty; both deny the pain of emptiness; and both are impervious to the possibility of impending death. I cannot profess to know how successful, or otherwise, the mystic's attempts at transcendence may prove, but I do know that all the anorexic is capable of transcending are her own immediate difficulties and that, in most cases, this achievement is comparatively short-lived. It may appear to an outsider that the anorexic is following a set pattern: self-confidence combined with an incredible energy is succeeded by despair and eventual collapse. But, as I have tried to show, the relationship between euphoria and depression is synchronic: depression does not follow euphoria, but is masked by it. The two co-exist, but in a state of war and, more often than not, depression wins.

The battle is a hard one for the anorexic—at first, hard-won, and then hard-lost. The main problem, as far as the body is concerned, is that nature will insist on reasserting itself. By nature I mean, first, the principle of survival which drives us to continue living and necessarily entails the ingestion of food; and, second, the principle of growth which transforms us from childhood to maturity and thence to old age. In normal circumstances these principles or facts of human life can be defeated by one means only: death. But although I wrote in my diary that I wished I were dead, I never seriously considered death—suicide —as a solution to my problems. Both Bruch and Minuchin show that a very small minority of anorexics commit suicide, but at the same time Bruch resists, as I do, the description of anorexia nervosa as "suicide in refracted doses."[2] Suicide and anorexia are by no means mutually exclusive phenomena, but in the typical case of primary anorexia nervosa suicide is simply not a factor, except perhaps when depression has won a particularly resounding victory, and the shame of defeat becomes unbearable. Nevertheless, the suicide, like the mystic, resembles the anorexic in certain ways. The American writer Leslie Farber has a great deal to say about "the life of suicide," which he insists, "must not be seen as the situation or state of mind which leads to the act, but that situation in which the act-as-possibility, quite apart from whether it eventually occurs or not, has a life of its own."[3] And although suicide is a conscious act, whether it is carried out (or even contemplated) "when the balance of the mind is disturbed," and anorexia is, at least at first, more of an unconscious process, I think there is a "life of anorexia" too, in which the act-as-possibility is never entirely absent.

If I admit that there is such a thing as a suicidal temperament, then I am forced to admit that there is also such a thing as an anorexic temperament. Failed suicides tend to try again, just as (failed) anorexics tend to relapse, and yet both can live for years without resorting either to self-destruction or self-starvation. Neither does the one tend to adopt the other's behavior as a replacement for her own more habitual strategy. In the light of Farber's observation, I should like to suggest that if one "has" anorexia nervosa, one does not need suicide. If the worst comes to the worst, says the suicide, I can always kill myself. And, in similar circumstances, the anorexic can always starve herself again.

Other similarities between the suicide and the anorexic seem to me to relate to the individual's reactions to an impinging world. Impinge- ment asks the question, where does the self end (or begin)? With it, we are back with the problems of identity, specifically those of projection, the process by which certain aspects of the self are seen as located in some object external to the self, and of introjection, the process by which certain aspects of external objects are seen as being located within the self; we are firmly back in the area of object-relations. In other words, we are back with the relationship between the self and significant others or the world in general. On reading the works of Sylvia Plath, who did indeed live the life of suicide, I have noticed that her comments on impingement often seem to coincide with my own feelings at the time I was anorexic. The examples are too numerous to quote, so I shall confine myself to two.[4] The first concerns her obsession with purity and her ambivalent attitude towards it. On the one hand, she writes, in *The Munich Mannequins*, "Perfection is terrible. It cannot have children." On the other hand, in *Tulips*, where the poet is ill and in hospital, the flowers, brought as a gift, "are too red in the first place, they hurt me," and the smiling faces of her husband and children in a family photograph "catch on to my skin, little smiling hooks." She declares, "I am a nun now, I have never been so pure." The flight is from the impingements of blood (the red of the tulips) and pain and from the complexities of close human relationships. It could also be read as a flight into death. Similarly, in *Fever 103*, she writes, "I am too pure for you or anyone./Your body/Hurts me as the world hurts God."

The two latter poems describe states of physical illness, but I think it is not unfair to quote them along with the former because all three only express in an overt form what is often expressed throughout her work: the connection between purity and superiority, the connection between purity and death. In anorexia nervosa, which becomes a living death, the same connections are prevalent, together with the same confusing implications. But it is in *Lady Lazarus* that the similarity between the life of suicide and the life of anorexia is at its clearest: "Dying/is an art, like everything else./I do it exceptionally well." On reading these lines I realized that, if the word "starving" were to be substituted for the word "dying," they could be read as a description of my own attitude at the time I was anorexic. There are the same elements of bragging, self-dramatization, childish defiance, and an assumption of the uniqueness of one's own behavior, all combined with a heavy sense of irony. I, too, thought I was doing something unique and practicing an art exceptionally well. And the irony entailed in starving myself in order to survive was not altogether lost on me.

For me the poem also has a more elusive quality, which I have perhaps hinted at in describing the extract as self-dramatizing. I get the impression that the poet did not take death seriously, did not quite believe in it. It may seem ridiculous to suggest that a suicide does not believe in death, but there is a certain amount of evidence to suggest that some forms of suicide (usually referred to as "schizoid") are in fact attempts at rebirth. In this context, E. S. Shneidman and N. L. Farberow have something useful to say. And although I do not agree with them that either suicide or anorexia are attempts to "get attention," but rather attempts to get identity and wholeness, the following passages may serve to illustrate the paradoxical type of thinking which dominates both states of mind.

> "If anybody kills himself, he will get attention, I will kill myself, therefore I will get attention." Deductively, this argument is sound, but the fallacy is concealed in the concepts contained in the word, "I." Here the logical role of the pronoun is related to the psychology of the conception of the self.[5]

This type of suicide believes that he will survive his own death, witness the discovery of his own body, and participate in the reactions of others towards his death. The passage continues, "More accurately, it is not a fallacy in the words of reasoning, but rather in its fallacious identification. Hence we call it a 'psychosemantic fallacy.' " I see "psychosemantic fallacy" as a perfect description of anorexia nervosa—a disease in which the concept of the whole person is so confused, so dialectically divided, that "I" can at the same time be choosing to live, as the self, and choosing to die, as the body, however unconscious those choices may be. And I would agree with Schatzman that "possibly one day we shall speak of *linguasomatic* or psycho*semantic* not psychosomatic illnesses."[6] The point I am trying to make is that both suicide of the schizoid type and anorexia nervosa involve a denial of reality which depends upon an acceptance of a split between self and body, and is only possible through paradox. A paradox is, among other things, a linguistic device, and can be used by the anorexic as the most expressive one in the language of her symptoms. As such it is neater than the confusion presented by a reality which can be seen as not belonging to the self; or as perhaps belonging to the self; or as, if belonging to the self, equally incapable of assimilation by it or separation from it.

Death must represent one of the strongest impingements of reality, and perhaps the most confusing for the confused self. But although the schizoid suicide and the anorexic both deny the reality of death, it seems to me that they do so for different reasons and in different ways. I have already stated that I discovered death at the age of six, and also that I never considered suicide as a possible course of action. In view of my evident misery, both at the onset and towards the end of the disease, the two statements may at first seem irreconcilable: I was desperately unhappy and had known for years that death can put an end to everything, including unhappiness. But, to return to Shneidman and Farberow's "psychosemantic fallacy," "We believe that this confusion or ambiguity may indeed occur whenever the individual thinks about his death, whether by suicide or otherwise. It may arise because he cannot imagine his own death."[7] I knew what death was, but I still couldn't imagine it. My knowledge, or rather realistic apprehension of it, at such an early age came from a coincidence of circumstances.

First, my pet rabbit died; one morning I found it stiff and cold in its hutch, for no apparent reason, and I was told that it was dead. It was buried in the garden with all due ceremony, and all I knew or felt at the time was grief that I should never see my beloved pet again. But some days later I realized the full truth of what had happened. My parents were discussing some incident in the past and, when I joined in the conversation to ask some question, they told me, as they often had on similar occasions, "Of course, that was before you were born." The innocent words suddenly filled me with horror: there had been a time before I was born, a time when I had not existed, a time when I *lacked individual consciousness*—this last being the most horrifying notion. But it was only when I was in bed that night and unable to sleep that I realized the meaning of my horrified reaction; there would be another time, after I was dead, when I would not exist, when my consciousness would be extinguished. And although such an eventuality was beyond my imagination (like trying to envisage infinity) and utterly unacceptable to me, I still knew it to be true. For long periods throughout my childhood I was afraid of going to sleep, afraid of the extinction brought by sleep. Although I dreamed and could thus distinguish sleep from death, although I woke up again each morning, the fear remained, and my sister's death only served to strengthen it. If I had killed myself, I should have known perfectly well what I was doing. I had none of the schizoid suicide's delusions about being able to survive my own death. Of two prisoners in jail, one may hang himself, the other go on hunger strike: the former is committing a positive act, the latter an act of passive resistance. The two acts embody differing attitudes towards life and death. For me, suicide would have been too active an act. My rejection of death was less a denial than a postponement of the recognition of its ultimate reality.

Death, like sexuality, is a biological fact, but anorexia nervosa entails the denial of biology, and in particular the notion of biology as destiny. When I was anorexic I postponed the idea of myself-as-mortal in the same way as I postponed the idea of myself-as-sexual-being. In the idealized world of childhood, to which I was trying to get or get back, neither death nor sexuality existed except as unwarranted intrusions, and all was a paradisal oneness, where to be individual and autonomous meant the same as to be accepted and understood. There was no separation anxiety, which in itself is a paradox, involving both the need and the fear of separation. Perhaps it is a universally irresoluble paradox, but it is one of particular importance for the anorexic. Death, like sexuality, exacerbates separation anxiety, each emphasizing the conflict between the individual and the universal, as well as all the conflicts inherent in object-relations. Each reiterates the question: where does the self begin or end? For me, death, like sexuality, was an aspect of the adult world, with which I felt myself incapable of coming to terms. But although I scarcely, if ever, thought about sex, I wallowed in thoughts of death, utilitizing them, rather than death itself, to bear or deny my increasing depression instead of taking steps to put an end to it.

To bear and deny depression at the same time may seem like yet another paradox, but my diaries testify that somehow I managed to do both. Even as I was recording my triumphs over a hostile and alien world, I was also expressing such sentiments as, "Oh, it's not even worth writing down—the same, usual, dismal, tedious, boring story." The plethora of adjectives points, again, towards self-dramatization, and it is clear to me now that I used this device as a means of bearing depression in general. What I did was to make a virtue of my misery. I sank into a kind of Romantic melancholy, which I could feed and sustain by reading Keats, Shelley, Tennyson, Matthew Arnold, and (above all) Byron. I could apply their larger statements about the futility of life to the smaller futility of my own, at the same time identifying with them in the literal sense and recognizing the irony inherent in any such identification. I could enjoy being "half in love with easeful death," or telling myself, "I have not loved the world nor the world me," or agreeing that, "our sweetest songs are those that tell of saddest thought." Literature has its uses. And I could turn out imitative verse which expressed similar sentiments. Melancholy cheered me up. It also helped me retain the image of myself as someone special, set aside from the throng, this time because of superior talent.

That I only half-believed in this self-image—and even that is probably an overstatement—was a circumstance I tried desperately hard to conceal, both from myself and others. Farber sums up the whole process:

> While despair means literally the loss of hope, the movements of despair
> are frantically directed towards hope; but the hope born of despair may turn
> to the prescription of the isolated will. Spurning the self-illumination
> arising from humility, despairing hope concerns itself pridefully with
> certainties. Even the certainties of hopelessness may paradoxically appear
> as a form of hope, promising to make reasonable what is unreasonable,
> namely hopelessness itself. [8]

I know that as I became more and more anorexic, I also became more and more despairing and, at the same time, because of my stubborn, isolated will, more and more determined to deny my despair by finding solace in despair itself. Even then I knew in a way that despair underlay my behavior, but I wouldn't have been able to take the consequences of its admission. I didn't and couldn't see it as a progressive condition which was bound to culminate in some sort of breakdown or breakthrough.

At first the physical symptoms of the disease were easy enough to deny: outwardly, I was fit, healthy, energetic, and never felt tired or hungry. In short, I was a walking, running, bouncing miracle. But gradually those symptoms had to be admitted and faced up to. The first to gain recognition was fatigue. In my diary I recognized it almost from the beginning, probably because I made no connection between it and non-eating, but seemed to have ascribed it to being overworked academically or being hounded into sporting activities which I resented for their profound pointlessness. I voiced my resentment openly, but my fatigue was confided only to my diary and to those of my friends who already knew that I was in the habit of getting up and wandering around at night. The truth is that I was suffering from insomnia: a full stomach is more conducive to sleep than is an empty one. The thinner I became, the more difficult I found it to be comfortable, even when lying in bed. Whatever position I adopted seemed to be the wrong one, and it was possible for certain parts of my body to be relaxed and at rest only at the expense of certain other parts. If I lay on my side, my shoulders and hips gave me particular trouble; if I lay on my front, my back ached; and if I lay on my back, the springs of the mattress dug into what little flesh I had left. At the time I attributed this discomfort to my surplus energy, and not to my thinness. I couldn't lie still, and found my oblivious companions both irritating and enviable. To lie awake hour after hour, while they were all so deeply asleep, became unbearable to the point of claustrophobia.

At first I would go for short walks, lasting perhaps half an hour, and then return to bed sufficiently impressed with my own daring to be able to relax into sleep. But as the anorexia progressed, my walks became longer as well as more frequent and, if I decided to follow the perimeter of the school grounds, could last for up to three hours. The times are noted in my diary and, if they are accurate, I must have survived for several days in succession on as little as one or two hours' sleep per night. This was obviously not a state of affairs which could continue indefinitely and, although I knew as much at the time, I couldn't will myself into sleep. Rather, I was willing myself out of it. Authority had decreed when I must sleep and when I must not, just as it had decreed when and how much I should eat; it was my business, in my bid for autonomy, to reverse the decisions of authority. I didn't deliberately set out to become an insomniac, but such an attitude fits into the general anorexic pattern, and should be seen as a part of it. My nocturnal adventures had become an addiction, being in themselves part of a larger addiction—that of non-eating.

But even I couldn't will wakefulness with complete success, and the events of those nights soon began to affect my day-time behavior. When I wasn't dozing off in chapel, I was having difficulty in keeping awake in class and, to a greater extent, during prep-time, when I was supposed to be working alone. School chairs tend to be even less comfortable than school beds, and I found it impossible to sit still for long—a fact which didn't endear me to irritable teachers, expecially those who also resented my "witty" (i.e., irrelevant) remarks. Nowhere in my diary do I mention this physical discomfort, and even now I can't remember it as amounting to pain, although I do remember the school doctor drawing the matron's attention to the extensive bruising on the softer parts of my body. What I did complain of was restlessness and the inability to concentrate. Alone, I could hide my inability, force myself to concentrate and to finish any given piece of work to the best of my ability, no matter how long it took me. In class, it was less easy to convince others that I was coping not only adequately, but brilliantly.

Increasingly, I was baffled by what was going on, and kept silent, only to be rebuked for not trying or for adopting a disdainful attitude. The truth is that I kept on having mental lapses, during which I could hear every word that was being spoken, understand the meaning of each word and even of some phrases, but couldn't make these disparate utterances add up to anything that made sense. Often I could see no connection between a remark made by one person and the reply given by another. It was not as though other people were speaking a foreign language, but rather as though they were using the English language as the basis of a code to which I had somehow lost the key.

Given my reputation for intelligence, I hardly dared confess my lack of comprehension. On the one occasion on which I did so (according to my diary) the other girls laughed, and the teacher became annoyed, accusing me of being deliberately provocative. My diary records the incident in a tone of self-righteousness, omitting to mention my feeling of incompetence. Instead, around this time, I tended to express feelings of impatience and boredom. I don't doubt that I—in my tenuous superiority—was impatient both with the school routine and the people around me, but I don't think I was bored. "Boring" is a convenient portmanteau word for adolescents to use in describing anything they find alien or frightening. And I think I was beginning to become frightened. I had regarded the English language almost as my own private possession, something which was mine by right, and now it seemed that I was going to have to fight to hang on to it, as I was having to fight for everything else. It seems ironic that, in my struggle towards meaning, I was faced with its loss, hit with its loss, in the place where it hurt most.

At home I slept better. There was no need for me to get up and prowl around while the rest of the family was sleeping because I could read all night, if I wanted to, and if I didn't get up until the middle of the day, no one seemed to mind very much. There was altogether less to be frightened of. I wasn't watched closely; I had opted out of the (sexual) competition with my sisters; and some of my eccentricities were tolerated on the grounds that my presence in the house was only temporary and, in the long run, of little relevance to its essential life. In other words, some measure of independence was granted me. But for this there was a price to pay: when I wasn't being ignored completely, I was being made fun of, especially in regard to my physical appearance which was frequently compared to that of a twelve-year-old boy. I should point out that the comparison was no aberration on the part of my family. I had very short hair, always wore jeans, sneakers and an anorak (being perpetually cold), and strangers would often mistake me for a boy—my younger sisters' younger brother. I found this mistake hurtful: more specifically, I didn't regard it as a source of amusement. The fact that I was anorexic, rather than odd-looking, was never openly discussed, and no steps were taken to halt the disease. Although these omissions suited me at the time, I have since found them incredible to the point of doubting my own powers of recollection, but when I checked recently with my sister, she confirmed their accuracy. I assume that my parents, preoccupied with their own affairs, thought that if my appearance and eating habits were ignored, they would, like all other unpleasant circumstances, eventually revert to normality.

The importance of my schoolwork was still stressed, especially by my father, while that of any form of social contact was given no consideration. I had no money to go anywhere or do anything. Here I was bored. The blank pages in my diary testify as much, and in addition that I was too apathetic to continue recording just how bored I was in the periods between my bouts of organizing activity. So the superficially more relaxed atmosphere at home did nothing to modify my anorexic behavior. Whereas at school I felt harried, browbeaten and driven to surpass, at home I felt neglected, devalued, and isolated. The drive to surpass had originated and was maintained from home; my sense of neglect and isolation was a partial consequence of belonging intermittently to a cohesive community. None of it hung together. My mental lapses in class were, as well as being the result of fatigue, a metaphor for what I felt about my life in general. At home my anorexic behavior sustained me: it was the only consistent factor in my life, the only thing that made sense. I could look forward to going back to school, astonishing everyone with my further weight loss, and engaging in battle with true adversaries—those who would fight back.

Certain forms of discomfort, certain forms of boredom, can be ignored or at least tolerated by means of diversion. But one of the oddest things about the anorexic is her ability to tolerate two deprivations in particular which others find quite intolerable, namely, cold and hunger. During the whole time I was anorexic, there is only one reference in my diary to feeling cold, and that was when the school heating system failed. In the first stages, the first winter, I don't remember feeling cold at all; or, at least, I don't remember that I suffered from cold any more than anyone else did. On the contrary, my hyperactivity helped to keep me warm. Outside, I would always walk briskly, urging on my more sluggardly companions, or walk along walls, rails, edges, like a child, delighting in my ability to balance myself.

On the lacrosse pitches my behavior took a similar turn. Whereas before I had more or less ignored the game and engaged myself in gossipy conversation with whoever was playing opposite me, I now began to act out a parody of the ludicrous pastime in which I found myself, tackling everyone in sight, yelling for the ball to be passed to me, jumping up and down, and generally getting in everyone's way. At home, I would go on long walks, which were less the contemplative rambles I had previously enjoyed than frantic attempts to keep the body going, to keep the machine working. No one else walked quickly enough for me, so I went alone and was able to indulge in yet another secret activity—climbing trees. I enjoyed physical exercise, but I also enjoyed the thought that I was getting away with the sort of behavior commonly considered inappropriate to a sixteen-year-old girl. Even indoors, where vigorous exercise was impossible, I would insist on open windows, explaining that lack of fresh air made me feel sleepy. I suppose that at school, where I had so little sleep, this assertion was true. If I had admitted to cold in any of these instances, I should also have had to admit that my fund of energy wasn't limitless. I should have had to admit to fatigue. But the fact remains that, while other people were shivering and in obvious discomfort, I felt impervious to cold. Needless to say, this discrepancy served to boost my sense of superiority.

As the disease progressed, however, cold became more and more difficult to deny. I would wear extra layers of clothing and pull the sleeves of my sweater down to hide my white, numbed fingers. I told myself that I didn't feel cold, that I felt nothing, that I had "shut off my nerves." This last phrase, used in my diary, is a revealing one: cold wasn't something imposed on me by anything as trivial as the outside temperature; it was something which could be controlled from within and by myself alone. My self wasn't my body. And cold was a property of my body—some tiresome thing which was nevertheless now completely under my control—and not of my self.

During the last summer of the disease, when I weighed under 80 pounds, I must have been perpetually cold. While my sisters wore sundresses, their backs and shoulders bared, I swathed myself in jackets, scarves and gloves. And still, I couldn't admit, even to myself, that I was cold. It seemed to me at the time that I was doing something other than trying to keep myself warm. What I felt I was doing, as I dressed my shivering body in layer upon layer, was protecting myself. If I went out without my battered old anorak, I simply didn't feel safe. I am not denying the truth of this feeling: to feel cold is to feel unprotected and each is a metaphor for the other state. But it seems clear that I was diverting the feeling of cold, which pertains to the body, away from the physical and into the psychological realm, where alone I believed myself to exist. My behavior must have seemed as absurd to others as my physical appearance which, with only the goose-pimply face visible, was pathetic.

My mother told me that I was cold because I didn't eat enough. Whatever the objective truth of this assertion, it could have been formulated on purpose to infuriate me, and I denied both halves of it. I did eat enough—if anything, too much. And I wasn't cold—I just liked wearing my anorak because I was fond of it and felt comfortable in it. Those were my spoken replies to my mother, but my unspoken one was that it was up to me, and not to her, to decide when and to what extent I was either cold or hungry. If I had admitted to being cold, I should also have had to admit that I was hungry, and this was something I was incapable of doing—if only because I didn't believe it to be true. To admit to hunger would have been to admit to my disease, and so be robbed of it. And at that point I should have endured anything to prevent such a theft. I was miserable with cold, but although I was prepared to admit that I was miserable, I wasn't prepared to admit that my misery had any connection with cold. My anorak served as armor in more than the literal sense: it protected me, as anorexia protected me, from the confusing impingements of reality as defined by others at home or at school, and who could not even agree among themselves, on my behalf. But in fact I was, in failing to come to terms with this total reality, only creating further confusion for myself. It would be too simple to say that I was always cold and hungry, as I appeared to be, at this latter stage of the disease. The truth is that I could no longer tell whether I was cold or not, hungry or not.

Most people know when they are hungry and will eat, more or less, accordingly. Bruch contrasts this fortunate majority with both the anorexic and the obese person, neither of whom knows how to gauge the state of her own stomach or assess what is a reasonable requirement of food for her own bodily needs.[9] The obese person cannot recognize that her stomach is full, nor the anorexic that hers is empty. It is easy enough to see how someone, especially someone who has suffered a childhood of poverty, can be led to fear of emptiness, of not getting enough to eat, of starvation itself, and so in later life to stave off or compensate for such a fear. And indeed obesity is a disease of the poor rather than the rich. It is perhaps less easy to see how someone from a privileged background can be led to seek emptiness as a physical state, when it is obviously such an unpleasant, even painful, one. Repletion is probably a more pleasurable state for most people than is emptiness, and its metaphorical implications are now widely understood: to be well-fed is to feel safe from poverty and death; it is to engage in an enjoyable activity; and it is to feel loved, if only by oneself. But the metaphorical implications of emptiness are less clear. Because it is both difficult and painful to maintain one's stomach in a state of emptiness, we cannot doubt that there are powerful psychic motivations for sustaining such an activity, which is not only abnormal, but directly contrary to both physiological and social pressures. Mara Selvini Palazzoli has found that, this psychobiological sensitivity invariably goes hand in hand with a remarkable *elan vital*, a passionate though suppressed love of life, a "sthenic spur" which alone explains [the anorexic's] heroic defence reactions. Let me add that it is this very spur . . . which has made her choose anorexia in preference to, say, toxicomania or obesity, two conditions that spell surrender to her own greed.[10]

It is, I believe, this same "sthenic spur," or determination to survive as a self-defined individual, which causes the anorexic to reject suicide —another form of surrender—and to choose the more arduous life of self-starvation, not in order to die, but in order to live and go on living.

Like Bruch's patients, I denied hunger and the pangs which accompany it. As the disease progressed, the denial became easier. In the earlier stages I knew the denial to be conscious and saw it as being some sort of test of my will. Later, when I began to lose weight more rapidly, I would dream frequently (probably almost every night) about food and eating. The food was always of the type that anorexics tend to shun—solidly starchy and savory peasant dishes, followed by mounds of sweet, creamy puddings and richly decorated chocolate cakes. The feasts took place out of doors, in convivial company, with the sun shining benevolently on us all. In the dream I would savor each delicious mouthful slowly, and share in general comments on the pleasure of what we were doing, or, indeed, on any other topics of conversation. But I would wake up, startled and guilty, horrorstruck that I had somehow managed to allow myself to get out of control. The relief which followed the realization that my conduct had been "only a dream" was always tinged, however slightly, with regret.

It seems to me that these dreams were not only manifestations of hunger, but that they also evinced a desire to be normal and part of the natural world. Clearly I connected eating with the beneficence of nature (the sun, the products of the earth) and with friendship, companionship and community. I must have known that those were the very advantages I had been denying myself in denying myself food. Food is to the body what friendship and community are to the psyche, and the world of nature to the integrated personality expressed as body-and-psyche. In my dreams I was admitting the full implications of my habit of self-denial, that is, that it amounted in effect to life-denial. I was also admitting that "I" was not a separate entity from my body, that we were both one, and both in need of nutrition.

But in waking life I ignored the implications of such a "sthenic spur," and continued to deny its existence. At that time I could only eat alone. My nocturnal escapades sometimes included visits to the school kitchens, where I ate bananas, leaving a mound of their skins conspicuously on one of the tables, and quantities of ice cream, which I scooped up in handfuls, defiling the common stock with the unhygienic touch of my individuality. Now I think of an animal or a small child depositing its excreta in the wrong place so as to annoy its owner or parent. I ate like an animal too—furtively, quickly, and as if in fear of discovery, but without enjoyment. It is clear that there was a vengeful aspect to this behavior, and one that was heavy with oral aggression. I think that in my secret eating I was saying, speech also being an oral activity, all the resentful and hostile things I wanted to say about the school and about my life in general. My secret eating was expressing what my secret writing (a misplaced oral activity) could not: my hatred towards those who oppressed me, my desperate sense of isolation. It was also expressing, on the most literal level, my determination to survive.

However, this behavior was short-lived, and when I dropped it, my dreams began to change. I still dreamed of food and the convivial, outdoor feast, but I no longer took full part in the proceedings. I would talk and laugh with my companions but withdraw, lapsing into silence, when I was offered any food. Then, at once, I would wake up before I could allow myself to touch a mouthful. In other words, my guard was now so strong that I would wake myself up rather than allow myself to eat, even in a dream. In waking life it was too strong to allow me to indulge myself in secret feasts, and I no longer felt any desire for them. By this time there was no need for me to deny hunger: I felt none. I could talk lengthily about food without longing for it, and at home I could cook meals without tasting and without my mouth watering. Food was still interesting material, but orally neutral, like cloth or paint or clay.

Occasionally the sight or smell of it nauseated me, and I found certain smells, like those of bread or sugar or chocolate, overpowering. But what really disgusted me was the sight of other people eating. It seemed to me shocking that they should engage in such a crude, almost obscene activity in public, and I would watch them with fascinated repulsion. The whole world stank, both literally and metaphorically, and I withdrew fastidiously from it. In this way hunger, in the sense of the desire for food, gradually disappeared, and I was no longer lying to myself or others about its absence. But I was still denying emptiness.

The most obvious connotations of emptiness are the helplessness and hopelessness to which I have so often referred and, in addition, a general sense of worthlessness. An obese person can strive to overcome such feelings by overeating and so gaining size, weight and (subjectively speaking) importance. And so it might seem at first that the anorexic is striving to maintain worthlessness. However, this is clearly not what is going on in anorexia nervosa, although I do believe that emptiness is being used as a metaphor. It is, in the first instance, a metaphor for that portion of the sense of worthlessness which cannot be denied, whatever the anorexic's outward behavior is saying to the contrary. To the obese person, emptiness is a space which must somehow be filled, overfilled, in the attempt to deny its existence. It seems to me that the implication in such an attitude is that the space *can* be filled—it *is* possible—and that this is therefore a more simple and perhaps less courageous attitude than that of the anorexic. For her, the dreadful underlying fear is that the space can never be filled: any such attempt would be futile, and so the best thing to do in the circumstances is to accept that the space exists, and to turn this fact to advantage. In her paradoxical way, the anorexic is facing up to the truth implicit in her own convictions.

That she sometimes has bouts of overeating in no way contradicts this assertion: after each one she is overcome by self-disgust and depression, and her sense of futility is confirmed. Minuchin's description of the anorexic as one who takes upon herself the burden of familial conflicts and the internal conflicts of those around her indicates that the anorexic "sees" what is going on within and among other people in a very special way. Without realizing it, she is facing the otherwise unadmitted truth about father's inability to assume responsibility, or mother's suppressed craving for power, or whatever the problems happen to be in her particular environment. And in doing so, she is internalizing, that is, she is filling herself with what does not rightfully belong to her. She cannot tell what belongs to her and what does not. As I see it, she is, in a sense, full, and so her own emptiness can be ignored or pacified. But, in another sense, she is full only of other people's emptinesses, and so her own remains, mingled with theirs and therefore all the more difficult to deny. But, in order to survive, in order not to be engulfed by it, she must deny it. And at the same time, she must distinguish her own from that which belongs to others, separate it, examine it and, if necessary, cherish it, as she must cherish anything which tells her who she is, anything which belongs to her alone.

I can well believe that at home I was going through some such process for many years before I became anorexic, as well as during the course of the disease itself. I felt my parents' anxieties about both their own and their children's lives so keenly that they became my own, quite against my will, and I had to fight to reject them. But I cannot honestly say that I find such an analysis applicable to my attitude towards the school authorities. As far as my own case is concerned, the scapegoating theory, delineated above, describes only a portion of the truth about emptiness. For a start, it doesn't cover the aspects of emptiness which I consider to be of most relevance to anorexia nervosa, that is, its peculiar meaning for females rather than males. Both Fromm and Erikson see it as woman's basic fear, bound up inextricably with her anatomy and, more specifically, her role in the sexual act. In describing the differences in anxieties about sexual function, Fromm describes the man's as fear of failure to pass a test, whereas the woman's lies in that of being "left alone," of not having control, of dependence on the man.[11] I have already emphasized the importance of control and independence as factors in the anorexic process, so I shall now quote Erikson to illustrate the relation between emptiness and being left alone, and the relevance of both to anorexia nervosa:

> The fear of remaining empty (oral) or being emptied (anal) has a special quality in girls, since the body images of the girl (even before she "knows" her inner anatomic arrangements) includes a valuable inside, an inside on which depends her fulfilment as an organism, a person, and as a role-bearer. This *fear of being left empty* and, more simply, that of *being left*, seems to be the most basic feminine fear, extending over the whole of a woman's existence.[12]

The famous experiments carried out and observed by Erikson at the University of California indicate that such arguments may amount to more than outmoded Freudian theorizing. To oversimplify: very young children of both sexes were given similar sets of building blocks with which they were asked to construct some sort of dwelling. The boys—the future architects of tower-blocks, perhaps?—built tall (phallic) structures, whereas the girls built low-rise structures, round and enclosing an open space in the middle. Of course various conclusions can, and have been, drawn from these experiments, but I think that they bear out Erikson's theory about the connection between women and inner space. The anorexic cultivates emptiness (and being emptied, through purgation, etc.) and at the same time denies it—or, at least, denies its pain. If emptiness, like passivity, is seen as an identifying characteristic of womanhood, we can see that the anorexic recognizes and even values her own (potential) womanhood, while at the same time denying it. I would therefore agree with Mara Selvini Palazzoli's contention that the anorexic, despite her apparent rejection of womanhood, is also showing "a keen desire, however distorted, to become an autonomous adult,"[13] and, indeed, an autonomous woman. But to the anorexic, that last phrase is a contradiction in terms: autonomy and femininity have been shown to be irreconcilable. And yet she cannot surrender either of them completely. Just as she uses passive resistance in order to overcome her own passivity, so she uses her empty stomach to overcome her own emptiness. Emptiness is both a cause and a result of passivity, and can be seen as its physiological epitome. The picture of the rejection of femininity is thus brought into sharper focus.

Erickson connects the fear of being empty with that of being left, the fear of abandonment. Fromm connects the fear of abandonment with the frustration arising from a necessary dependence upon others. Both are referring specifically to the woman's role in personal relationships, but it seems to me that their comments could just as easily be applied to the role of children in relation to adults. Children are similarly dependent, frustrated, and in fear of abandonment. I would surmise that at adolescence such fears remain with girls, whereas boys are diverted towards other anxieties connected with proving themselves. The conventional way of looking at adolescence does, at any rate, emphasize some such division. If this view is correct, I can only conclude that I was saddled with both sets of anxieties and, in addition, that there are more and more adolescent girls today who are finding themselves in the same position.

On the one hand, I had been instructed, both implicitly and overtly, to prove myself and, in Fromm's words used to describe typically male anxiety, to demonstrate what a "good performer" I was. In doing so, I should prove not only my own worth, but that of my immediate family, of the people of Lewis and of all MacLeods everywhere. Needless to say, I never felt myself equal to such a mission. If human communication were a simple matter of reciprocally exchanged words, if words had no resonances beyond themselves, I might have been proud to be cast in such a role, and either self-confident enough in my ability to fulfill it, or else realistic enough to modify my directives and declare myself in favor of some more modest role.

But communication between parents and children doesn't work like that. Young children believe what their parents tell them, verbally or otherwise: there are no other sources of information. (At least, there were fewer when I was a child than there are today.) In my parents' expectations there was always an element of unspoken threat: you must do this, or else. . . . Or else what, I didn't know, except that it must be something terrible. And there was the unspoken assumption that, if I failed, I was letting the side down, disappointing my parents, hurting them. In believing my parents, I was forced into the position of not believing myself and of not believing in myself. I was brilliant and I was stupid; I was a credit to the family and I was a disgrace to it. In becoming anorexic, I was attempting to overcome this confusion, and for a while I partially succeeded. But the weaker I became physically, the more inadequate I felt. I existed in a state of permanent exhaustion, unable to eat or sleep, and unable to laugh or even smile. Engaged as I was in the struggle with myself, the struggle between my self and my body, other people had no real existence for me. I no longer believed them or believed in them, having to believe in myself as a matter of survival. But at the same time I dimly knew that they were somehow successful human beings and that I, I alone, was not. Depression, however ruthlessly suppressed, was inevitable.

On the other hand, I had also been instructed in what it was to be a woman and to function successfully in that role. If a boy has to prove himself a man by his performance, then a girl has to prove herself a woman by her attractiveness, her desirability. Through my mother and my sisters, this was the stereotype I had learned at home. But I considered myself to be unattractive, and in becoming so thin as to render myself totally undesirable sexually, I was saying, "I may be unattractive, but this is because I choose to be this way." At school the ideal of womanhood was based on the assumptions of a different social class: woman's life was service, the dispensation of charity, whether she was married and dependent, or earned her own living. The picture can hardly be described as a dynamic one. Rather, it encompasses the traditional passivity and the traditional secondary role, whether of helpmeet within marriage, or devotion to duty and to "those worse off than oneself" outside it. I felt that I was more in need of charity myself than capable of dispensing it. In becoming anorexic, I was saying to those who were in effect my social superiors, "I can contribute nothing to the community; look how little I have/am." In both instances I was declaring my unwillingness to compete and my fear of competition. This was not only because I would rather have won than lost anything, but also because, winning being unlikely, I would rather have opted out altogether than lost. I was running the wrong race; I should never have been entered for it in the first place. Such an attitude is, of course, typical of the "oral personality," as classically defined in the annals of psychoanalysis, and I think it is no coincidence that anorexics, who are almost invariably subject to heavily competitive pressures, should choose eating as the focal point for expressing the resulting conflicts.

I am sure it must be possible for an adolescent girl to reconcile the male and the female sets of anxieties. All I am saying is that it wasn't possible for me. And as the disease progressed, all the anxieties became more difficult to ignore—necessarily, because I was growing older and, in my regressive, pre-pubertal state, more of an anomaly than ever among my peers. It was, in other words, becoming more and more difficult to postpone the future. And although I knew by then that I was wretchedly unhappy in comparison with other girls of my age, this was still what I wanted to do, because however joyless and painful the present might be, the future could have been even worse. It was still my task to fight for the present, although that task was becoming less appropriate daily, and to maintain the *status quo* which I had made for myself, and which was the only place where I belonged. Again, depression was inevitable.

The conflict between male and female anxieties was compounded by the conflict between the disparate values of home and school—two closed systems at variance with each other. It was to some extent a class conflict and, although I am glad to have had what is commonly regarded as a "good education," I must seriously doubt the wisdom of the County Council's charitable and well-intentioned scheme. As so often in this story of my own anorexia nervosa, I find myself arriving at the same conclusion, the same central statement: it could have worked for some people, but it didn't work for me. What was peculiar about my own circumstances I have already tried to describe in the hope of finding and revealing some useful clues. Clearly my history is not one of overt cruelty towards me on the part of others; neither is it one of extreme neglect, restriction or hardship. It is rather one of lack of understanding on the part of others, of ignorant if well-meaning insensitivity towards a sensitive child and adolescent. It is a history of confusion and of a last-ditch defense against confusion. According to Peter Lomas, there are

> two main theories about the psychological origins of mental illness: the "defence theory" and the "confusion theory." . . . These two theories are, to my mind, unquestionably correct and compatible. What has so far prevented them from becoming assimilated to each other is not only the fact that in the field of psychotherapy, differing theories do not readily and happily intermix, but that each theory tends to take sides (without this necessarily being apparent) in the eternal dialogue between youth and age. Whereas the defence theory, which stresses the child's unwillingness to adapt, is on the side of the adult, confusion theory, by focusing on the failure of the family, is on the side of the child.[14]

Although I don't think I was mentally ill for most of the time I was anorexic, I find Lomas's remarks illuminating in my own case and pertinent to anorexia nervosa in general. I don't want to take sides between myself-as-child-and-adolescent and the adults around me: the issue is not that clear-cut. Still less do I want to take sides between differing schools of psychotherapy. But I do want to stress that "confusion" and "defense" are two of the key words in anorexia nervosa, and that the disease could serve as an illustration of Lomas's belief, being a process in which the two concepts are inseparable and mutually reinforcing.

I "chose" anorexia rather than mental illness as a defense against confusion. But towards the end of my anorexic period I think I was verging upon mental illness in the sense that even those who disbelieve in it might accept, that is, I had become out of touch with reality as perceived by others and unable to cope with demands of everyday life. I had begun to feel that there was some sort of glass partition between me and the rest of the world. Until then I succeeded in holding the impinging world at bay as well as in the desperate attempt to establish my own identity, but it was only at a bitter cost to myself. Nothing moved me, and Coleridge's line, "I see, not feel, how beautiful they are!" sums up my eventual attitude to all that I had ever found valuable or of emotional significance. I could see, and I knew what was the appropriate emotional response to, say, a beautiful day, but I couldn't feel it. This is depression.

In 1968–9 I wrote a novel, *The Snow-White Soliloquies*,[15] which tells the story of a girl who endures a living death in a glass coffin, and is trailed around the country in a glass vehicle by a motley collection of social misfits (dwarves) under the supervision of a sinister authority-figure called Doc. The theme was based on that of the Snow White story, and the authority-figure's name derived from the Walt Disney version of it. When questioned at the time, and for some time afterwards, as to what the novel was "about," I would reply vaguely that it referred to a period in my life in the 1960s, when I was married to a successful pop star and spent much of my time traveling up and down motorways, lulled with anti-depressants and sitting, an immobile non-person, in the back of a sealed, silent and chauffeur-driven Rolls-Royce.

This was, of course, true as far as it went. But it was only later, when I was forced to admit that, at the time of writing, I had begun to become anorexic again, that I realized in addition how closely the central character's circumstances resembled those of anorexia nervosa. Later still, my realization was confirmed for me when I read the following statement from one of Bruch's patients: "I am completely isolated, I sit in a glass sphere. I see other people through a glass wall, their voices penetrate to me. I long for being in real contact with them. I try, but they don't hear me."[16] This is just what happens in my novel: the girl, Snow White, listens to the life-stories of her companions but, try as she may, she can neither comment nor reply in kind. The total symbolism of the novel shows that it is "about" alienation, depression, and the inability to cope with an ever-increasingly impinging world: it is in the details that the references to anorexia are revealed. For instance, Snow White is fed by means of tubes, a procedure which, unknown to me at the time, is still a common practice in the treatment of anorexics. She resists being fed because she is afraid that she will swell up and become too big for her coffin. Her eventual release can only come about through the death of Doc and the proof of her recovery lies in her willingness to participate in a wedding-feast. Sex, symbolizing conjunction, is reconciled with food, symbolizing conviviality and an acceptance of the natural world. The problems of object-relations have apparently been resolved. But not quite. Before she can eat, Snow White assumes the authorial voice, insisting that the other characters are her inventions, and that it is she who has always held the real power.

At no time during the writing of *The Snow-White Soliloquies* did I make any conscious connection between its contents and anorexia nervosa. This is the point (not self-advertisement—the book is out of print) of referring to my own work in such detail, and it is one to which I shall return in discussing the treatment of anorexics, in particular their apparent imperviousness to psychoanalysis and their liability to relapse. At the time of writing I was too taken up with the present to make any but the vaguest connection with what had happened to me in the past. This seems strange to me now because I feel sure that if I had been presented with the image of the glass coffin when I was well into the depressive phase of anorexia, I should have recognized it instantly. But I am not so sure that I should have recognized what I recognized unconsciously at the time of writing: that I was in a state of helplessness, the helplessness of being a non-person. It seems more likely that I should have denied depression, helplessness and, above all, being a non-person. But in fact, towards the climax of the disease, there was very little of me left, in more than the physiological sense.

As life in general was unreal and remote—seen through a sheet of glass—so my own suffering seemed unreal. The sight of, say, a field of corn interspersed with poppies on a sunny day didn't move me; the spectacle of a woman who had slipped and fallen in the street didn't move me—either to sympathy or to ridicule. Why, then, should I be moved by cold or a stomach cramp? What was going on in my body was as unreal, as devoid of meaning, as were the events in the outside world. The two were part of one whole, a whole of which "I" was no part. "I" had shrunk to a nugget of pure and isolated will whose sole purpose was to triumph over the wills of others and over the chaos ensuing from their conflicting demands. Distinguishing between will of the first realm, which must "to some degree remain impenetrable to inspection," and will of the second realm, which is both conscious and utilitarian, Farber suggests,

> The problem of will lies in our recurring temptation to apply the will of the second realm to those portions of life which will not only not comply, but that will become distorted under such coercion. Let me give a few examples: I can will knowledge but not wisdom; going to bed but not sleeping; eating but not hunger . . . self-assertion but not courage . . . reading but not understanding. . . . [17]

Some similar process is going on in anorexia nervosa: the conscious will has to be supreme because the anorexic has to be in complete control. Because of her fear of loss of control, her essential helplessness, any control that is less than complete is no control at all. But of course the human body is simply not capable of being subject to such control over prolonged periods. The anorexic who has achieved her emaciated state is faced with two choices: she can relax her control and surrender her will, thus admitting defeat; or she can allow herself to die of starvation, thus gaining her paradoxical victory. There is a point of despair at which she is forced to choose between life and death, however unconscious that choice may be. Without the aid of any sort of therapy, and certainly without the sympathy and understanding which should attend it, I managed to opt for life.

6

RECOVERY

In cases of anorexia nervosa the problem of recovery is first and foremost one of recognition. People who suffer from other psychosomatic conditions are often all too ready to recognize and even dwell upon the fact that they are in some way ill. But this is exactly what the anorexic does not or will not recognize. Because to her there is nothing abnormal in her condition, the question of recovery is at best an irrelevance, and at worst an unmerited attack upon her integrity. In a way, she is right. There is no evidence whatsoever to suggest that anorexia nervosa is an organically induced disease, although it does inevitably produce the organic symptoms characteristic of undernourishment, and all attempts to treat it by purely organic methods have proved singularly unsuccessful.

The anorexic continues to deny the organic symptoms of her disease because she knows, however unconsciously, that they are only secondary, a result rather than a cause of her predicament. If she is capable of being a stubborn liar, the anorexic is also capable of a certain stubborn honesty in the sense of being true to herself, the self which has somehow been mislaid and/or starved, and which she must find and nourish again. In feeding the body, the wrong part of herself is being nourished. It is the true, the buried self which is in need of real nourishment, and the more the wrong part (the obvious, visible body) receives, the likelier the right part is to remain buried and die of starvation. The body is being fed at the expense of the self.

It is important to recognize that this split between body and self is a fundamental tenet of anorexic thinking, and that recovery must necessarily entail a closing of the gap, a healing of the split between the two, however imperfect the reconciliation may be. In view of this fact, it is hardly surprising that attempts to make the anorexic eat, as if her non-eating were a purely organic ailment, have almost always proved, in the long run, to be counterproductive.

The administration of tonics, vitamins or hormone therapy (to induce menstruation) has been found to have no effect on the patient's eating habits, let alone her underlying psychological condition, and the last may even lead to uterine haemorrhages.[1] Neither does hospitalization in itself provide an answer to the problem, even the immediate physiological one. Force feeding, either by means of tubes, or based on a system of rewards and punishments according to the number of calories consumed, tends to make the anorexic feel coerced, and so more rebellious than ever.

Some of these systems are more humane than others. All of them involve a great deal of bed-rest, which in theory seems like a reasonable recommendation for the exhausted anorexic, but can in practice be seen by the patient, or used by the hospital, as a form of punishment in itself. In some cases, the patient is fed a light diet at first, with the number of calories being gradually increased over the weeks. According to the extent of her cooperation, she will be allowed to get up for a few hours, bathe, make phone calls or receive visitors—privileges otherwise denied to her. Other regimes may consist of a steady diet of 3000 calories per day combined with complete bed-rest until the patient has reached "target weight." These may or may not involve psychotherapy, family therapy or occupational therapy. If they do not, they are probably useless as long-term strategies for recovery. A life consisting of nothing but eating and sleeping, with the additional perk in return for docile behavior, is not an adult life and, in my opinion, is also less than a human one. It reminds me of a battery animal being fattened up for the kill.

When these strategies fail, as they so often do, more punitive methods are put into action. An ex-nurse from a well-respected hospital gave me the following outline of the treatment (which she assured me was normal practice) of a particular anorexic patient. The woman, in her early twenties, had been anorexic for three years, and had failed to respond to the orthodox rewards-and-punishments system, so she was left alone in a small room which contained nothing but a mattress on the floor. Meals were presented regularly. If the patient consumed a certain number of calories, she was allowed a page of a newspaper to read; a larger amount would be rewarded with a magazine or a bath; and a finished meal earned her the reward of being able to see her mother. When I pointed out that the mother was probably the last person she wanted to see or should see, I was assured that, on the contrary, there was always a very strong bond between anorexics and their mothers. My attempt to explain the ambivalent nature of this bond was met with a mixture of non-comprehension and disbelief. So I wasn't surprised to learn that the patient had later been classified as chronic and incurable. And it is clear from the work of Anorexic Aid and the Anorexia Counselling Service that such idiotic and harmful methods of treatment are still in wide use.

Some anorexics will rebel openly and resort to self-induced vomiting, or lie, cheat and steal in order to obtain laxatives and so counteract such forms of treatment. [2] Others, perhaps more cunning, soon realize that if they eat, if they gain a little weight, they will be released from the hospital; and, once they are released, they will be free to resume their former eating habits. To the anorexic, hospital must seem like a prison where she is being punished for seeking autonomy by being deprived of what little autonomy she has managed to find. Insulin treatment (which in itself makes her fat) combined with anti-depressants and/or tranquilizers seems to me a particularly cruel form of treatment for the anorexic: it reduces her to a doped, drowsy, will-less creature, a *thing*—the very condition she has been trying to avoid. But, if such treatment is an insult to the integrity of the personality, what is there left to be said about ECT (Electro-Convulsive Therapy or "shock treatment")? It has often been advocated and administered in the treatment of anorexia nervosa, but I would consider both the advocators and the administrators guilty of crimes against humanity. I would also consider them guilty of a dangerous naiveté: do they really consider the human psyche such a simple entity that it can be set on its "right" course by the application of a few thousand volts of electricity? Hospitalization may often be necessary as a life-saving measure, but there is no excuse for such drastic treatment being administered to young people who have no history of endogenous depression, especially when it is generally recognized that no one knows how and why ECT "works"—if and when it does.

Although some forms of drug treatment may be necessary in the short term to alleviate organic symptoms which seem to be leading towards death, I fail to see how they can have any long-term effects without the back-up of extensive and intensive psychotherapy. And I would agree with Bruch that the organic approach is "useless, if not harmful."[3] As I have already stated, I myself received no treatment, but I feel sure I should have rebelled against hospitalization or, indeed, any form of treatment which I should have considered coercive, namely, all attempts to treat my condition as a purely organic one. Any of them would have robbed me of myself. As it was, my "spontaneous" recovery was at first and mainly organic. And I resented it deeply and bitterly.

My recognition that there was something abnormal about my behavior and condition came slowly and in three separate stages, or, rather, incidents. While I was anorexic, I had always considered myself to be extraordinary rather than abnormal. The difference between the two concepts can be seen more easily if we convert the two words into their antonyms. To be ordinary carries connotations of being dull, boring, unimaginative, unadventurous and, in school parlance, "stodgy." Like many a non-anorexic adolescent before and since, I despised ordinariness (and would have applauded Billy Liar's anger and disgust on reading his mother's description of herself as "an ordinary housewife"), while seeing it as a state to which most people were condemned.

Two constant refrains run through my diaries of the anorexic and immediately pre-anorexic periods: "If only I could meet some interesting people!" and "If only I had someone to talk to!" I craved the company of others who were far above the common run of the people I tended to know, either at home where those around me seemed to be exclusively concerned with the petty details of their own daily lives, or at school where no one ever did anything "because it's never been done before." I had been told repeatedly that ordinariness was not my habitat, but it was a state into which I was betrayed at adolescence by my body. Other girls may have blossomed, but I was plain and ordinary, a dumpy little thing to whom no one would have given a second glance. To me, this was an unbearable indignity and, moreover, a downright lie. I was *not* ordinary—Mummy and Daddy had told me so—and, if people couldn't see that for themselves, then I should have to show them the truth by purging myself of all traces of ordinariness. If I had not been cloistered in a boarding-school, if I had had any money, if, indeed, I had been someone other than myself, I might have gone in for extraordinary clothes and make-up, or dyed my hair an extraordinary color like a punk teenager of today. As it was, I had no such resources, and was left face to face with the chief source of ordinariness—the body itself.

To be normal, on the other hand, carries connotations of health, happiness, competence and, above all, good relationships with others. I didn't despise normality. On the contrary, I envied it while regarding it as something beyond my reach. Normal people fitted into their environment and, being able to grasp the rules which governed it, were also able to accept their roles within it and play them out with good grace. But I was an anomaly, both at home and at school. At home, I was a freak, mocked and isolated, longing for friendship and companionship. At school, I was a freak, having increasingly less in common with the other pupils who all seemed to have the backing, financial or emotional, of their families, whereas I felt (rightly or wrongly) that my family grudged me everything, even my very existence, and, far from planning my future with me, would have been ready to disown me if I had failed to gain a university place. It seemed to me that whatever I did, in either place, I could do nothing right, could please no one. If I had been accepted either at home or at school, it would probably not have been necessary for me to become anorexic; the accepting environment might have made the rejecting one easier to bear. There would have been some refuge for me somewhere, some niche, however small, in which I could cultivate my openly acknowledged true self. As it was, I had to reject both places as they had rejected me.

But to retaliate in this way was only a partial solution to the problem: the question remained as to why I had been rejected, why I could do nothing right. I simply didn't understand it, and in attempting to do so, I was forced to the conclusion that the cause must lie not only with my rejectors but somewhere within myself—perhaps only within myself. One of my recurrent dreams in the immediately pre-anorexic period took place in a court-room where I was on trial for a murder I had never committed. Nothing I said or did (and there was no one else to defend me) could convince either judge or jury of my innocence. I was condemned, capital punishment being in operation at the time, to death. Similarly, in waking life, it seemed to me that I had done nothing to merit such lack of faith in the person I felt myself to be, and so the fault must lie in what I was, rather than in what I had done or not done. It lay in some inescapable part of myself, rather than in my behavior. But, try as I might, I couldn't find this part. It was far too abstract and mysterious, whereas my body was concrete, accessible, obviously imperfect, and therefore "chosen" as a scapegoat. The choice was not, of course, a conscious one, but through it I managed to deny abnormality, while cultivating extraordinariness: I was no freak, but a person of rare appearance and accomplishments. Up to a point, this pathetic, last-ditch strategy could have worked, and in theory did work, but in practice there is a very thin line between extraordinariness and abnormality. And it was only when I could see how tenuous it was, and how easily it could be smudged or broken, that I was able to take the first step towards recovery.

This happened one hot summer day in 1956 on a platform at Newbury station. I had gone to the station because I knew it was the only place where I could find a proper weighing-machine, that is, one with real weights which could be moved around, and was used for weighing luggage. It was a matter of common knowledge that the machines at Woolworth's or outside chemists' shops, where you put a penny in the slot, were not to be trusted. And at home there were no bathroom scales, such things being considered mere vanities. Neither were there any laxatives, and I had no money to buy any. The idea of forcing myself to vomit didn't (and never did) occur to me. And so, since the end of term, I had had no means of checking up on my weight. It had become clear to me that there was no possibility of cheating, as there had been at school, and that in order to stop myself from gaining weight, I should have to adopt the straightforward method of giving up eating altogether. My resolution was meant literally, but I must have succumbed occasionally, because I remember feeling swollen and polluted after consuming what, to others, would have been a negligible amount of food. By this time I had lost all sense of proportion, and would imagine that the swallowing of a bite of an apple, a crumb of cheese or a spoonful of soup constituted overeating. Having no means of objective verification, I panicked, convinced that I was getting fatter and fatter. And the more convinced I became, the more depressed. Somehow I had to reassure myself.

Newbury was four and a half miles from the village where I lived and, having no bus fare, I decided to walk there and weigh myself. So I set off, wrapped in all my usual layers, telling myself that if I walked quickly and determinedly enough, I might manage to shed all the extra pounds I had accumulated in such numbers that I had reached the dreaded and odious weight of 112 pounds. I drove my body on, allowing it no respite until I had reached the town. By the time I had reached the station, I was sick with apprehension, with a kind of stage-fright. Making sure that I was unobserved, I stepped on to the machine, only to find that, fully-clothed as I was, I weighed 80 pounds—or, naked, as I reckoned, 78 pounds. My first reaction was one of overwhelming relief, but it was followed at once by a feeling of bewilderment. How could I have got it so wrong? Instead of having gained 28 pounds, as I had feared and imagined, I had lost almost 7 pounds. I didn't *feel* 78 or 80 pounds: I felt much larger: I felt fat. And yet the weighing-machine—the only one I could trust—couldn't lie. I must be thin. I was thinner than I had ever expected or even hoped to be. Just for a moment I was frightened. Once more my body had assumed control by behaving according to its own laws, not mine. But the moment passed. I wasn't fat, I didn't weigh 112 pounds, so what was there to worry about? I had been reprieved from my obsessive fears of the past few weeks. I found a two-shilling piece on the platform and took the bus home, feeling that providence had smiled upon me. But in the days that followed I couldn't quite rid myself of my bewilderment: it pointed to a colossal misjudgment on my part, a failure of intellect. And it was my first intimation that all was not right, that there was something abnormal going on in the workings of my mind.

The second intimation, which followed shortly afterwards, was less directly concerned with weight. I was sitting in the branches of an apple tree in the garden, pretending to be absorbed in a book (as I remember, it was *Sons and Lovers*) but in fact feeling a tired kind of loathing for literature and the printed word. My mother asked me to come down from the tree, saying that my behavior was ridiculous, that the neighbors could see me and think that I was loony. I ignored her. I hated her. But I think she was trying to get through to me, because, instead of insisting that I do as she asked, she changed the subject and began to talk about the flowers in the garden. At the far end there was a solitary, full-blooming sunflower standing against a red-brick wall and a head above it. It was the only one that had survived. My mother remarked on its beauty and nobility, adding that she had a special fondness for sunflowers, and explaining that the name was derived from the way in which the plant turned its face slowly round throughout the day, following the movement of the sun. Still I didn't respond, didn't even look at her, although I found myself listening to her. Then she began to quote Blake's poem,

> Oh sunflower, weary of time
> Who countest the steps of the sun,
> Seeking after that sweet golden clime
> Where the traveller's journey is done.

She spoke in an awed, hushed voice, rather posher than her usual one, which I found rather foolish. But the words themselves filled me with nausea, pain and anger, all at once. They seemed to express my own weariness, my own longing to be something or somewhere other than I was. They also brought home to me the fact that although I, like the sunflower and all other organic things, was living out a natural cycle, I had somehow shut myself out, cut myself off from nature, of which I was inevitably, inescapably a part. Of course I couldn't have expressed such a revelation articulately at the time: all I knew then was that something was wrong, and that that something was probably my emaciated state. My mother went on to quote the rest of the poem,

> Where the youth pined away with desire
> And the pale virgin shrouded in snow
> Arise from their graves and aspire
> Where my sunflower wishes to go. [4]

It was then that the shock of recognition came. I knew that pale virgin shrouded in snow: she was none other than myself. I was cold, untouched and untouchable, and in my grave where I didn't want to be. I wanted to be warm and in the sun, touched by the sun, and a part of normal life, rather than apart from it. But I didn't know how to do it; I didn't know how to arise from the grave, to lose my pale virginity of flesh or psyche, and to follow my aspiration towards a life which I had now begun to see as preferable to the half-life in which I was imprisoned. Again, I was frightened, but this time depressed as well, more depressed than ever.

It was not the poem itself which jolted me, because in fact I paid no attention to its true meaning, extrapolating from it only what seemed to apply directly to my own condition. It was rather the circumstances: the mysterious power of the words being spoken in the actual presence of the sunflower and in my mother's voice. The sunflower made Blake's words concrete in a distorted manner, just as my body expressed in concrete terms the mess of confused emotions and miseries which existed within me. I was and was not the sunflower. I was the sunflower in the poem, an abstract, artificial sunflower, and not the sunflower rooted in the garden. And yet the sunflower in the poem *was* the sunflower in the garden, and the sunflower in the garden *was* the sunflower in the poem. It seemed right and proper that this should be so. And it seemed wrong that I should be able to make only one half of the identification. The wrongness wasn't a matter of morality, but rather of aesthetics. Perhaps, after all, the world moved in some sort of rational harmony, to which I had been deaf, having perceived it as being beyond my comprehension. And perhaps I, too (ways of perceiving the world being metaphors for ways of perceiving the self), was capable of harmony and wholeness, as I had been in my early childhood. Fear had brought with it a sliver of hope, as well as the recognition that I was now, by contrast, a jarring, disjunctive thing. But

I couldn't acknowledge that hope then. It was obliterated by an agonizing sense of loss. I wanted to weep, as I hadn't wept for years, but I did no such thing. Making no comment on my mother's/Blake's words, and affecting to remain unaffected by them, I returned dry-eyed to my book.

If someone other than my mother—an actor speaking on the radio, perhaps—had recited the poem, I doubt if it would have had the same effect on me. Although my condition had not been mentioned, it seemed to me that she was recognizing it with sympathy for the first time, that she wanted me to return to normal for my own sake and not for hers or the family's, the neighbors', or the world's; she wanted to point out to me the full extent of what I had been missing. Perhaps she did. But perhaps I only believed what I wanted to believe, what by then I needed to believe, because death (still felt as psychic rather than physiological) was encroaching daily, and it was as horrifying in its own way as life had been and still was. Perhaps my mother was being very clever in referring to the snow-shrouded virgin, instead of telling me directly, as she had done so often before, how awful I looked and what a pathetic creature I was. And then, again, perhaps the whole incident was a fortuitous accident. What I do feel sure of now is that my recognition of myself as others saw me had to come from her, from her first and so, perhaps, from her alone. She had to acknowledge that she was deeply involved in my anorexic condition, even if she were incapable of acknowledging how or why, as indeed I myself was at the time. And I think that in some half-conscious way she must have known as much herself, because she kept on trying to get through to me in the same indirect manner, even in the face of my apparent and consistent lack of response. At any rate, she was also responsible for my third and final step in the process of recognition, a step directly concerned with eating.

Plums were my mother's favorite fruit, and I suppose they are among the most sensuous and fleshy, the most feminine. It must have been a good year for plums, because the ones my mother bought were large and luscious and plentiful. One day she offered me one. But she did so in a manner which was at once casual and ritualistic. For a start, she was breaking the rule against eating between meals, and so engaging me in some sort of complicity with her, which excluded the other members of the family. What she did was to pick out what seemed to her the two choicest plums and show me the bluish bloom on their dark purple skins. Then she washed them both, and wiped them dry before showing them to me again, handling them delicately, as if they were precious works of art. The bloom had disappeared, the purple shone, polished. Taking a bite out of one, she handed me the other. I accepted it. I think I accepted it because it hadn't been offered to me as food but as an aesthetic object, and my suspicions had been temporarily allayed.

I held the plum in my hand, enjoying the look and the feel of it, and it wasn't until I held it to my mouth, and I could smell it, that I realized that it was food and intended to be eaten. At once I felt a wave of extreme nausea which I found myself trying to control or subdue. I couldn't let my mother down. And yet I had to. I thought, Oh, my God, there must be something wrong with me when the smell of a plum, a beautiful object, can sicken me so. My mother was watching me. She must have seen the sudden horror in my face because she asked me, "What are you afraid of?" I remember staring at her, rigid now with fear, torn and unable to move between two conflicting emotions. I couldn't answer her. "It won't kill you," she said. I didn't know whether it would or not, but I had to find out. I was being challenged. Nauseated as I was, I bit into the plum. I forced myself to chew it, to swallow it, and, very slowly, to finish it. I don't know how many plums my mother ate during that time. But my nausea had vanished. To my surprise, I felt neither full nor fat, but strangely relieved, strangely comforted.

That moment marked the beginning of the end of my anorexic behavior, but it should not be seen as the moment of my recovery from the disease. After recognition, the next step in the process of recovery is understanding, and I was very far from any such thing, as I was to be for years. I relinquished my non-eating pattern only very gradually and tentatively. A struggle was still going on in me, a struggle between the desire to be normal and thus accepted, and the desire to cling on to my disease as the one expression of my individuality. I was sent away to Scotland to stay with an aunt and uncle for a couple of weeks, and I

suppose I must have eaten more or less normally while I was
there—away from both home and school—because when I came back I
weighed nearly 98 pounds. Everyone congratulated me on my appearance, telling me how much happier and prettier I looked. I received
their congratulations with mixed feelings: they were humoring me, and
yet I should have liked to believe that they were sincere. How could I
possibly look prettier, when flesh was essentially ugly? And yet I had to
admit that people no longer stared at me and shrunk from me as if I
were a freak. How, also, could I be happier, when I was less myself? Yet
I had to admit that I was no longer in a state of deep depression, and
found it easier to communicate with other people. The world had
become an altogether friendlier place.

Because of this and because I felt so much better physically, being no
longer dogged by cold and hunger, I allowed myself to eat, as I thought
minimally, for the remainder of the summer holidays. But I was still
unable to judge for myself how much I should eat. My misjudgment
was now veering in the opposite direction, and when I returned to
school for the autumn term, I weighed 104 pounds. The matron was
delighted. "Just right," she said. And my friends congratulated me on
my recovery from such a devastating illness.

But I was horrified—on two levels. First, I disagreed on principle
with the matron's assessment of what was "just right" for me: how could
she know better than I did? The fact that her assessment was backed up
by people who seemed to wish me well (that is, pupils rather than
teachers) might have helped me to accept it. But I was convinced that I
was already too fat and, once the process had started, all that would
happen to me was that I would go on getting fatter and fatter. In other
words, even if my weight at the time *was* "just right," I had no idea how
to maintain it. Control was being taken from me and handed to my
body: it no longer did what it was told. Then I saw what had happened
to me during the summer holidays, and this realization constituted the
second and more bitter level of my horror. I had been duped, deceived,
betrayed, especially by my mother. I had been tricked into eating,
through seeming sympathy and the pretense that I should feel better for
it. But I didn't. I felt worse. I had allowed myself to be treated as an

idiot, and had therefore lost my integrity. After the long, lonely struggle, I had finally been defeated, had finally given in, almost without knowing what I was doing. And I despised myself for it.

My experience shows that getting the anorexic to eat is only half the battle—if that. It is, of course, an essential part of it, and in some cases must temporarily override all other considerations in order to save lives. But in less extreme cases it is always a delicate matter. If, as I believe, coercion in the form of force feeding or the administration of appetite-inducing drugs, is inadmissable, then some gentler, more reasonable form of persuasion must be used instead. Coercion is both cruel and counterproductive, but other forms of persuasion may involve deceit on the part of the doctor or therapist, and anorexics, though accomplished liars themselves, are hypersensitive to hypocrisy on the part of others. They also tend to be susceptible to an almost paranoid fear of betrayal and humiliation. And so the immediate problem, that of non-eating, is generally approached in an indirect manner.

The lunch sessions described by Minuchin and his colleagues are an exception to this general psychotherapeutic trend in that they are designed to combine the direct and the indirect approaches to eating. Their particular form of therapy begins with a lunch to which all the members of the family, including the anorexic herself, are invited, along with either one or two therapists. The first general discussion of what is seen as the family predicament, rather than that of the anorexic alone, takes place over a simple meal of hot dogs, sandwiches or salads. Everyone orders whatever food she/he pleases from the hospital canteen, and a discussion of family habits and preferences begins before its eventual arrival.

When the food does arrive, and everyone but the anorexic starts to eat, certain attitudes begin to emerge from other members of the family towards eating, meals, food, and to the anorexic's disparate behavior. "If the patient does not eat," says Minuchin, "it makes sense to look at the field of family transactions around eating."[5] While observing these transactions, the therapist can utilize one of two strategies—those of overfocusing or underfocusing on the food itself. Minuchin concludes that overfocusing seems to be more successful in cases of younger anorexics, where the girl's refusal to eat can be described in terms of disobedience towards or lack of consideration for the parents, and therefore inappropriate to the parent-child relationship as a whole. Maybe. Maybe a few very young, very timid anorexics would fall, or seem to fall, for this sort of approach. But I don't believe a word of it. To emphasize an anorexic's feelings of guilt towards her parents seems to me like a recipe for future disaster, that is, for future relapse. Underfocusing usually consists of the therapists engaging the parents in conversation, perhaps about their own relationship, to the exclusion of the anorexic who, finding her parents thus "distracted," can then allow herself to eat.

Minuchin and his colleagues have found that a surprisingly large number of anorexics have begun to eat again after the first lunch session. But the sample they quote (eight patients) is far too small to mean very much, and they themselves admit that the resumption of eating in such circumstances should not be seen as a quick cure, because the results do not last unless the family treatment continues. In fact, all they claim in this context, is that "the goal of the session is to transform the issue of an anorexic patient into the drama of a dysfunctional family,"[6] rather than the more immediate one of getting the anorexic to eat.

But the fact that she so often does so at the first lunch session is interesting. It seems to me that it is important, not only for the anorexic to eat, but to be able to do so in the company of other people. Both my recurrent dreams and the fact that I could bring myself to eat more or less normally when away from both home and school, point to this conclusion: the anorexic will eat in the right, that is, the sufficiently unstressful context. It is a conclusion which Minuchin and his colleagues seem to have to arrived at by default. Nowhere do they stress the importance of eating as a shared experience, let alone as a ritual communion into which one (the anorexic) is admitted without question and on equal terms with the others (the family and the therapists). Both the lunches and the other family sessions described in Minuchin's transcripts are far from being convivial occasions, but if one reads between the lines and those of the therapist's comments, it is possible to see how the anorexic can be led to a new sense of communication and community, both less hypocritical than before, and thence to a new sense of communion. Oddly enough, I, as an anorexic, see Minuchin's method as paradoxical: it works to remove hypocrisy in being hypocritical in itself.

The hypocrisies involved in the transactional patterns within the family are shown up ruthlessly by the therapist, often in a manner which I find both brutal and distasteful. People are reduced to tears or to screaming at one another on the provocation of the therapist. Maybe these inhibited and inflexible people need to be able to break their own family rules by weeping openly, or exchanging insult for insult, instead of accepting each one in martyrish silence or exaggerated hurt. But they are still being bullied. When they are congratulated on their "performances," they are being patronized. And when they are left to be observed through a one-way mirror, they are being spied on. As far as I can gather from the transcripts of these sessions, every member of the family, whether adult or not, is being treated as a rather unintelligent child who can never hope to understand the mysteries of the hieratic profession whose skills are being utilized for the family's own good, and must therefore not be questioned. Sometimes these "skills" seem to resemble those necessary for the performance of a Whitehall farce, with staged arguments held between therapists; one therapist mysteriously leaving the room and abandoning the family to his colleague (he will, in fact, be observing them through the one-way mirror); or both therapists leaving the room for a quick consultation (also staged) out in the corridor.

Perhaps I am being insularly British in finding such a carry-on typically American in its crassness. The aim of the treatment is to speed up the therapeutic process and hence recovery. To this end, no stone is left unturned, no wound unprobed. It is not the probing I object to, but the speeding-up, and the cliché-ridden way of labeling, discussing and dealing with emotional attitudes as if they were a rather ugly wallpaper which can be stripped away and replaced without much difficulty by one with a more pleasing pattern. Throughout my reading of these transcripts, I kept asking myself, how can these people stand to be treated in such a manipulative and condescending manner? The answer became clear soon enough: they would do anything to help their daughter/sister, to save her from imminent death and, being helpless to do so themselves, they had placed all their faith in what seemed to be the only hope left for them. But when I asked myself how the anorexic (typically resistant to coercion, manipulation and recovery itself) could put up with the family therapy described in these transcripts, I had to look for different answers.

I came up with two. Most of the patients treated successfully by Minuchin and his colleagues had been anorexic for a year or less. And most were in the young anorexic age group (that is, sixteen or younger), some being as young as nine or ten at the onset of the disease. In other words, the majority were not chronic anorexics, who are notoriously more difficult to treat. And, despite the early onset of puberty, the majority were still children, altogether dependent upon their parents and, with one notable exception as far as the transcripts are concerned, incapable of making decisions which would affect their own lives. It makes sense to treat girls like these as very much part of a family: they were all deeply involved in the family structure and had considerable difficulty in being able to envisage themselves as separate from it. But I am inclined to doubt whether similar methods would be as effective with older and perhaps more intelligent anorexics.

There is some evidence to show that the average age of anorexics in England is going up, and that the incidence of the disease in university populations is rising.[7] It seems most unlikely to me that an anorexic university student who had maintained her condition for some years would willingly lay herself open to the manipulative techniques employed by Minuchin and his colleagues. She would surely be able to see through the elaborate procedures devised by such an authority in much the same way as the hospitalized patient can see through what seems to her to be a plot engineered for the purpose of fattening her up. I was neither particularly old nor particularly advanced as an anorexic, but I feel sure I should not have been deceived, and would probably have looked upon the whole business with the lofty contempt which the anorexic reserves for those who are transparently stupid enough to attempt to change her behavior by devious methods, while failing to admire or even acknowledge her heroic stance.

Another problem, as far as the older anorexic is concerned, is the involvement of the parents. Many of these girls (or, indeed, young women) are not living with their parents, or, at least, not living with them all the time. Although the emotional attachment to the family may remain strong on the part of the anorexic herself, and even on the part of the parents as well, physical distance alters the pattern of family relationships. The parents may remain over-concerned or over-protective from afar, while the anorexic herself is trying to break away from them in order to gain some modicum of independence, but at the same time unable to be brutal enough to take the necessary steps achieved by her peers without the need for any action which their parents would be inclined to perceive as uncaring, ungrateful, re-jecting, and so on. Or the parents may have decided, quite suddenly, that once the girl has (more or less) left home, she has, equally suddenly, become an independent being. They may express regret at such an occurrence but, again, the pattern of relationships will have changed. The removal of the anorexic from the home environment will lead also to the removal of accessible and reliable parental support, which is essential to family therapy.

It is at these junctures of separation that the anorexic is least likely to want her parents to be involved in any sort of therapy, and most likely to be willing to undertake it alone. She may feel that the paradoxical pull towards and away from her family can only be resolved in their absence, when she has a better chance of being herself. Certainly I shouldn't have wanted my parents to be involved in my recovery on any formal level. I didn't want them to know what I was thinking or feeling about my condition, and if I had tried to express as much, they would have contradicted me and rebuked me for my foolishness. I feel equally sure that they themselves would not have wanted to be involved: anorexia nervosa was my problem, not theirs. The home truths of family therapy would have both hurt and angered them and led them into endless soliloquies of self-justification, which they would have expressed to each other, but probably not to me. In other words, they would have been hostile to, and perhaps scornful of, family therapy, being as they were more averse to self-exposure than they were capable of recognizing the possibility of my death. After all, reticent, respectable people don't discuss their private affairs with strangers like Dr. Minuchin. And after all I was a healthy, intelligent girl who was just going through some silly adolescent aberration, but would soon come to my senses. There was no question of death, no question of unhappiness: all I needed was "feeding up."

Attitudes such as these may have changed in the last twenty years or so, but I wonder if they have changed that much. Psychotherapy, in its varying forms, may have become more acceptable to the educated and/or middle classes, but it should be remembered that nowadays anorexia nervosa is not confined to those, and that the man in the street still regards "trick-cyclists" with suspicion, connecting them specifically with insanity, as even the most superficial study of popular humor will show.

I am not against family therapy. But I do think that the family is a less easy entity to define and isolate than the advocates of this form of treatment would have us think. Both Minuchin and Selvini Palazzoli take the nuclear family as the norm (ignoring the emergence of serial marriage, i.e., divorce and remarriage) and point to the importance of its weaknesses in the aetiology of anorexia nervosa. Selvini Palazzoli, however, stresses the changes which have overtaken such families in recent decades, namely, the diminution of the patriarchal role, and the tendency for wives to work outside as well as inside the home. These are changes which have led to tension between husbands and wives, whether the wife goes out to work or not. It is a tension which, although it reverberates throughout the family with an anorexic member, is seldom articulated or otherwise openly expressed. The change focuses on the position and status of wives and hence, inevitably, on the position and status of husbands. Selvini Palazzoli makes much of this change, but has found that the mothers of anorexics tend to be women who remain at home and generally resent their status as "just housewives." Some had adapted in a martyr-like fashion to this role, others in a tyrannical fashion which led them to expect an impossible perfectionism from their children, especially their daughters. In such a situation the adolescent girl is bound to question her own role, both in relation to other women in general and to her own mother in particular. The answers she finds (or approaches) must necessarily be confusing.

My own experience both confirms and contradicts the picture of the anorexic girl's mother as a woman whose main interests in life are her home and her immediate family. Until I was fourteen or so, my mother was a housewife with a large family—a full-time job which, although she was never tyrannical, obviously both taxed and frustrated her. In this context, two memories stand out. First, I remember refusing to carry out some mundane household task on the grounds that it was "her job." She replied, quite rightly as it seems to me now, that the task in question was no more her job than anyone else's. Second, I remember giving her what I thought was a wonderful birthday present: a gilt brooch from Woolworth's which spelled out the word "Mother." I had intended it as a kind of homage, but she refused to wear it, saying grimly (and again rightly) that "Mother" was not her name. On both occasions she was decidedly angry and, although her anger puzzled me, I got the message: she was telling me, a ten- or eleven-year-old girl, that she had some identity other than that of housewife and mother.

A third memory bears witness to the confusing implications of this message. I remember asking my mother in an oblique fashion, when I was twelve or so, if her lot in life was what I could expect for myself. Was it enough, I wondered, to grow up, get married, have children, watch them grow up, get married, have children, and so on? Wasn't there more to life than that? She surprised me by extolling the simple, everyday joys of motherhood as opposed to the riskier ones of achievement in the larger, non-domestic world. When I insisted that I wanted something more, she told me that I was doomed to disappointment and that I should think myself lucky if I ever found a man to marry me and be the father of my children. Being my father's daughter as well as my mother's, I found this a difficult message to assimilate. I hoped that she was wrong, and at the same time was afraid that she might be right. The fact that she later went out to work herself did nothing to dispel my sense of confusion.

Recently I spent a weekend at a gathering of families with an anorexic member, and I was interested to note that some of the women who worked outside their homes had received complaints from their daughters that they were not "proper mothers." It would seem that those girls had some notion, as I had, of what a "proper mother" should be, although it was impossible to tell how and from what source such a notion had arisen. At the same time they were refusing, in becoming anorexic, to be "proper mothers" themselves. It is not a role to be trusted, perhaps because it has been shown to be in itself either unrewarding or inadequate, perhaps because it is impossible to fulfill. In other words, it offers at once too little in terms of expectations and too much in terms of demands. Anorexics, being perfectionists, prefer to do things "properly" or not at all. For them, to be less than perfect is not to partake in the common lot of humanity but to be classed as failures—a fate to be avoided at all costs in order to fend off their deep-seated sense of worthlessness.

Selvini Palazzoli's approach to family therapy is, unlike Minuchin's, geared to the recognition of social change, and the way in which it affects transactional patterns within the family, whether the family chooses to accept it or reject it. It is interesting to note that the one case described by Minuchin (Loretta Menotti) which relates most closely to Selvini Palazzoli's findings as well as to my own case, concerns an anorexic who was a member of an Italian immigrant family. My family were not strictly immigrants, but there is no doubt that we came from a different culture—one which was important to my parents and, by the time I was adolescent, meant little or nothing to me. In my case the dichotomy was compounded by my being sent away to school and having to adapt to a culture which was different again—not just an English as opposed to a Hebridean culture, but an upper-class culture as opposed to a petty bourgeois one. If indeed these factors are important in the aetiology of anorexia nervosa, the problem of recovery becomes a very complicated one. Short of us all returning to a feudal system, we must regard social as well as geographical mobility as an incurable disease. Economic factors make it a necessity in Western societies, and one with which we can only try to come to terms, if we are to rescue the resulting casualties. I think Selvini Palazzoli is right in seeing the anorexic's family as one such casualty and the anorexic herself as the chief victim within it. And it is her awareness of these larger issues which differentiates her work in family therapy from that of Minuchin and his colleagues.

Family therapy is primarily about communication within the family, and it is not surprising that those who have worked with the families of anorexics have found the same sort of disorders in this area. Minuchin may discuss "enmeshment" and Selvini Palazzoli "coalitions," but their findings as well as their methods are remarkably similar. Selvini Palazzoli has found that family members tend to justify, modify or contradict whatever it is they may have to say—that is, they tend to qualify both their own communications and those of others. Generally speaking, each member was able to qualify her/his own communications coherently and only rarely by contradictory or violent behavior. But, as far as the qualification of the communications of the other family member is concerned,

> The *rejection* of messages sent by others is extremely common in families with an anorexic member. Very rarely will one member bear out what another has said, particularly about how he defines himself in the relationship. Contradiction is common . . . it is as if each member of the family reacted to the other's message in the following way:
> "I reject the content of what you say, even though I acknowledge your right to say it. And I also reject your definition of yourself (and myself) in our relationship."[8]

Define or be defined, as Szasz has said. When we envisage a family striving for self-definition, both as a unit and as individual members, his dictum carries even more weight, and it is not surprising that the rejection of messages from other family members could arise as a reflection of a similar rejection of messages from the outside world. The Selvini Palazzoli method of dealing with this central problem is similar to that employed by Minuchin. Two therapists take part in the family discussion, one joining in and reinforcing the family's definition of itself, while the second one remains silent. The silent therapist then asks his colleague to join him for a private discussion outside the room. When they return, the first therapist allows the second to explain to the family why he thinks his colleague is wrong. "The *rejected* therapist," Selvini Palazzoli tells us, "looks duly contrite, and, by acknowledging his error, *confirms* his colleague's message."[9] Because this tactic delivers a blow to the family system in showing a peaceful redefinition of a one-up-one-down relationship, she adds that it has "invariably proved effective." Unlike Minuchin, she provides no transcripts of interviews from which the tone of these sessions can be gauged, but it is clear that an element of farce remains, this time with the addition of a nice little piece of sexism: the rejected therapist is almost always a woman.

It is interesting that Selvini Palazzoli should have arrived at family therapy only after years of treating anorexics in isolation. But, for reasons which I have already outlined, I find this approach as partial, though not as inadequate, as the purely organic one. It must be remembered that not all anorexics are members of families in any regular sense at the time of their illness. It must also be remembered that anorexics tend to relapse, some for the duration of their lives. It may be a truism to say that each of us is ultimately alone, but I should like to reiterate it because it seems to me that the very real intrapsychic conflicts of the anorexic are in danger of being passed over or minimized in the current trend towards family therapy.

The best sort of family therapy does not, of course, operate in this way, being as fully concerned with the psychopathology of the ostensible patient as with that of the other members of the family. But it is the Behavioristic trend which worries me. It seems simple-minded to suppose that, once the rigid and enmeshed family structure has been opened up, once all its members (including the anorexic herself) have seen the light and so the error of their ways, the anorexic will be well on the road to recovery. Again, this may be so with younger anorexics who have the full support of their families, but anorexia nervosa has wider and more complex implications. The exclusive emphasis on the family context leaves two important questions unanswered, or, at best, only partially answered. Why does one person rather than another in the same family become anorexic? And why is the female body chosen so unequivocally as the locus of pathology? The answers to these questions must lie to a large extent within the anorexic herself, and any move towards recovery must attempt to answer them to the individual's own satisfaction. And so the possibilities of individual therapy should not be discounted.

It is difficult not to gain the impression from the literature on anorexia nervosa that individual therapy has been devalued because (among other reasons) psychotherapists do not like anorexics, and anorexics do not like psychotherapists. Anorexics are notoriously difficult patients, being suspicious, frigid, untruthful, uncommunicative and determined to hang on to their symptoms at all costs. The therapist, in turn, "finds it difficult to respond with sympathy."[10] Selvini Palazzoli's former method is based on allaying the patient's suspicions (and fears) that all the therapist wants is to fatten her up. Dietary problems are not mentioned at first, but the patient is told that her fasting is merely a symptom of some other, more deep-seated problem. I feel that this is the right starting-point: the anorexic may be surprised by the change in emphasis, but the therapist will only be expressing what she has long suspected without being able to put it into words; she may also begin to see her obsession with food in a new context and be able to displace it, if only slightly, from its central position in her thoughts. If she is a stable anorexic without severe personality disorders (as indeed most are) she will at once recognize the truth in what the therapist is saying, and will not feel that she is being tricked or cajoled, but treated with some honesty, as one adult by another.

Of course she will not admit as much to the therapist but, in spite of all the evasions, silences and stubborn refusals to comply, it is possible for therapy to proceed on this basis, as Bruch and Selvini Palazzoli have both shown. The balance to be struck is that between, on the one hand, the anorexic's fundamental mistrust of personal relationships which have so often proved to be symbiotic and destructive and so to be escaped by an adoption of physical symptoms, and, on the other hand, her equally fundamental longing for a good relationship with one other person who will understand her and accept her for what she feels herself to be. This balance could be called friendship, and although the anorexic is difficult, sometimes impossible, to befriend, I am sure that this is what she wants and needs. It is a relationship which does not make undue demands and encourages mutual respect rather than dependence. Anorexia nervosa may grow within the family context and be fed (overfed) by it, but to the anorexic, the most important member of that family is her mother. It is through her relationship—or lack of one—with her mother that her problems of identity and autonomy, as well as those relating to her own body, have arisen. In other words, anorexia nervosa is symptomatic of a (perhaps very early) failure of a one-to-one relationship.

It does not seem illogical to posit the establishment or restoration of a good one-to-one relationship as a hopeful approach to the recovery of the anorexic. That this relationship was originally one between two females is also significant. I would suggest that a female therapist is likely to be more effective than a male one. Certainly I should never have been able to talk to a man. And a reading of the work of Bruch and Selvini Palazzoli, as compared to that of their male colleagues, has tended to confirm this point of view.

The disadvantages of this approach are that it demands a patience which is almost superhuman on the part of the therapist; and that it is both lengthy and costly. After all, Selvini Palazzoli seems to imply, why spend years in session after apparently fruitless session, when twenty sessions of family therapy can promote a dramatic change in the anorexic's behavior? It is easy to see how anorexics can exhaust the patience of those who attempt to cure them. And it is easy to see how the apparent effectiveness of a quickfire approach to cure can inspire and convert anyone who has worked for years with anorexics, using more conventional methods with an increasing sense of hopelessness. But I remain unconvinced by such arguments. The process of recovery is necessarily a long one. It involves no less than the complete reassessment of a whole life, however short that life may have been, and the psychic rehabilitation of a mutilated human being. What the anorexic needs in general from any form of treatment is an understanding of herself, which will lead her to participate willingly and actively in the process of her own recovery. This understanding need not be psychoanalytically based and, as I shall explain, such a basis is generally neither necessary nor helpful. The one-to-one relationship with the therapist can help the anorexic to meet some of her more specific needs in a realistic self-assessment. Often they are the very needs which have not been met in childhood, needs which the mother was unwilling or unable to supply.

The therapist cannot, of course, act as a "mother-substitute" in the literal sense, and I would in fact think it better if any attempt at "mothering" were to be avoided: in the case of the anorexic, it is not an activity designed to promote friendship and trust between therapist and patient, but rather one fraught with all the love-hate, admiration-resentment confusions which have played such an important part in the onset of the disease. What I am trying to suggest is that the therapist can help the anorexic to identify what has been missing in her life of deprivation and self-deprivation, what are the gaps which have led her to her distorted view of herself, and in particular her view of the relationship between her self and her body.

For the anorexic, the central problem in realistic self-evaluation is often, in contradiction to the arrogance and apparent imperviousness of her behavior, the ability to value herself more highly. She may tend to overvalue (overtly, at least) certain of her character traits—such as strength of mind or scholastic achievement—while despising the lack of them in others. These lacks, which can be summed up as a feeling of the total weakness of the ego, are the very ones which she feels in herself behind her facade of diligence and hyperactivity. Now, it is a common-place that whereas the love of the father is conditional upon the good behavior and praiseworthy achievements of his offspring, the love of the mother is, ideally speaking, unconditional. If there is more than a modicum of truth in this axiom (and I am sure there are many mothers who would agree that there is), it can be seen that the anorexic is behaving like a person who has never experienced mother-love. She is behaving as if the world were full of fathers only, fathers who have to be impressed, pleased, gratified. I don't want to engage in the vexed question of blame, but I'd like instead to allow Erikson to answer his own question, "Is Mom really to blame?"

> In a clinical sense, of course, to blame may mean just to point to what the informed worker sincerely considers the primary cause of the calamity. But there is in much of our psychiatric work an undertone of vengeful triumph, as if a villain had been spotted and cornered. . . . No doubt both patients and psychiatric workers were blamed too much when they were children; now they blame all mothers because all causality has become linked with blame.[11]

It is not my intention to spot and corner villains, and I think that the distinction between causality and blame is an important one, which should be emphasized in order to avoid misunderstanding. An absence of mother-love in a child's early years may occur for various reasons —such as the mother's illness, the death of a close friend or relative, or the birth of another child—none of which point to frigidity or callousness on the part of the mother. I think it would be of some help to the anorexic if the therapist could advance such a reading of her behavior, without engaging in any heavily psychoanalytical explanation. The follow-through would be for the therapist to persuade the anorexic that love, friendship, acceptance, approbation and so on are not necessarily contingent upon diligence and achievement, any more than they are upon one's physical appearance. Such a persuasion is essential to the process of re-evaluation, and to the patient's newly-evolving self-esteem. It is surely more helpful to her as a would-be independent being to foster it within the context of a one-to-one relationship than within that of the family battleground.

Selvini Palazzoli suggests that the strengthening of the ego is the first step in psychoanalytical treatment, and further, that it is one which can only be taken when the patient has voluntarily made some remark about the authentic state of her feelings, which can then be used to reveal the constructive potentiality of the ego. It is clear from her exasperated tone that she has often waited a long time for any such remark to emerge. And in her opinion, it is only then that analysis proper can begin. Bruch more or less agrees as to the primary goal of individual therapy, concluding in addition that, "instead of dealing with intrapsychic conflicts and the disturbed eating function, therapy will attempt to repair the underlying sense of incompetence, conceptual defects and distortions, isolation and dissatisfaction."[12] But, if I read her aright, she is in favor of the therapist taking a more active part in this procedure, suggesting that she/he *evoke* the "awareness of impulses, feelings and needs originating within . . . the essential step in helping a patient develop a sense of competence in areas of functioning where he had been deprived of adequate early learning."[13] This is the sort of learning, I have suggested, that usually comes from the mother. It is she who first handles the child's body and monitors her/his bodily responses to the world. It is she who first fosters her/his sense of competence and self-confidence. But of course it is easier to identify such omissions and to see their connection with the symptoms of anorexia nervosa than it is to repair them.

Both Selvini Palazzoli and Bruch (among others) report that anorexics seem to be singularly unresponsive to standard psychoanalytical treatment. Selvini Palazzoli has found that patients who opt for it are rare, and that most terminate their treatment once the main problems underlying their symptoms have been identified, imagining that they are now capable of managing on their own. It is best, she adds, to agree with them rather than undermine their new-found faith in themselves. I would add that it is best to agree with them because they may actually be right. Bruch has found that "insight" into the unconscious conflicts experienced by the anorexic does not lead to a cure, but often to a devastating re-experiencing of the girl's early life, which may serve only to confirm her sense of inadequacy and inhibit true self-awareness. To have her thoughts and feelings "interpreted" by the therapist can frighten the anorexic, not only because they themselves can be frightening, but because she is once again being "told" what she thinks and feels. Consequently, feelings of helplessness and hopelessness are increased rather than diminished or eliminated.

Both writers suggest that one-to-one therapy, seemingly effective in its early stages, starts to break down once psychoanalysis—usually the next stage in the treatment—has begun. I can see why. Orthodox psychoanalysis separates patient and analyst: they no longer talk face-to-face, and the anorexic's sense of isolation is intensified when she talks (if she talks) into thin air, and is answered (if she is answered) by a disembodied voice. The analyst appears to the anorexic to be a person apart, objective and without warmth, an authority figure to be feared and resisted. The anorexic herself tends to feel like a specimen lying on a couch, once more a thing. In her terms, the relationship cannot be said to be characterized by friendship. "Unless there is an acceptance by the therapist of equality with his patient," Lomas has said, "the undertaking is jeopardized from the start."[14] I would suggest that this statement is more true in reference to anorexics than perhaps any other patients.

I have already suggested that one of my own novels is open to a psychoanalytic interpretation which indicates a familiarity on the part of the writer with the condition of anorexia nervosa. And I have explained that I was unaware at the time of the possibility of any such interpretation. My aim in mentioning those circumstances was to show

how deep-seated the conflicts are, how firmly rooted in the personality; it was also to stress that anorexia nervosa is essentially an unconscious process, in that no one sets out deliberately to become anorexic, but rather uses strategies which may lead to anorexia as a last-ditch stand against helplessness and hopelessness. It may be that the invasion of the unconscious by psychoanalysis is just what the anorexic is unconsciously seeking to resist. Like the body, the unconscious is private property. Once its processes have been brought into consciousness and examined in the light of rationality, they may be found wanting. They may seem ephemeral or unreal and unfounded; they might have to change or even disappear. To the anorexic, these eventualities may add up to another form of theft: not only will they rob her of her disease, but also of the possibility of using it again in the future, should the need arise. Such an attitude does, of course, ignore the constructive potentialities of psychoanalysis, but these are not always immediately apparent to the patient, who may only perceive attack and destruction. For the anorexic, both the body and the unconscious must be safeguarded against invasion; and they must both be kept in their proper place, that is, under firm conscious control, *her own* conscious control.

There are forms of individual therapy other than orthodox psychoanalysis, and both Selvini Palazzoli and Bruch have explored some of these. Selvini Palazzoli discusses (all too briefly) the contribution made by existential analysis to the treatment of anorexia nervosa. The main feature of existential (otherwise, existentialist-phenomenological) analysis is that it does not concern itself with causes, but with being-in-the-world. Its concept of man, the human being, is derived not from the clinical experience of Freud and others, but from the thinking of such Existentialist philosophers as Buber, Jaspers and Heidegger, who all attached a great deal of importance to the philosophy of communication. It is outside the scope of this book to provide either a description, however potted, or a critique of existential analysis. All I can do is try to indicate its relevance to the problem of anorexia nervosa. Selvini Palazzoli describes it as "psychopathology from the inside," as opposed to the Freudian version which catalogues symptoms and syndromes "from the outside," and she goes on to say that "it tries to analyse modes of being a specific person in a psychopathological world of self-realisation through abnormal symptoms."[15] In this sense, anorexia nervosa may be seen as an existential rather than a clinical neurosis: the anorexic is someone who can find no other way of being-in-the-world than through a process of self-starvation.

As Frankl points out, "Existential philosophy deserves the credit for having proclaimed the existence of man as a form of being *sui generis*. Thus Jaspers calls the being of man a "deciding being," not something that simply "is," but decides first "what it is."[16] In this sense, anorexia nervosa can also be seen as an existential problem, the anorexic having been deprived of her power of decision-making in general, and in particular, the very decision which Frankl describes: that of who or what she is. The aim of the therapist in such circumstances is to help the patient towards a state of being-in-the-world, which is at the same time her/his own world, a world with which she (in the case of the anorexic) can come to terms. But Lomas's description of the whole process is, probably because of his own critical attitude, the clearest I have come across (obfuscation being one of the characteristics of this particular school of thought) and is perhaps worth quoting in full:

> The "existential" or "phenomenological" school of thought . . . lays stress on viewing phenomena in a simple direct way that is not disturbed by a pre-occupation with underlying causes. In the context of psychiatry this means that the important question is *what* the patient is experiencing; *why* he experiences things as he does is secondary; the aim is to find one's way into the perceptual world of the patient, to see things as he sees them, rather than explain his behaviour in terms which have been brought in from outside his experience—such as "case history" or "environment" —and which are therefore inappropriate.[17]

In view of the comparative failure of orthodox psychoanalysis in the treatment of anorexia nervosa, it seems strange to me that the existential approach, which appears to be altogether more sympathetic and less rigid, should not have been applied more widely. It is endorsed to a certain extent by Selvini Palazzoli, and it is clear that she has used this form of therapy herself, but she devotes so little space to its discussion that she gives the impression of having rejected it by omission. However, she does give one example which I find significant in relation to the beginnings of my own recovery. Citing the case of Lena, "her ambivalent fear of life and death, her hunger and satiety, her fullness and emptiness—all reflecting the opposing pull of desire and panic," she goes on to describe a speech or statement she made to the patient, concerning the nature of the body, which generates life, but also decay:

> Life and death, flowering and fading, generation and putrefaction are inherent aspects of life and existence. The opening up of a flower and the ripening of the fruit are the starting-points of their eventual decay. But it is precisely because it precedes putrefaction that the blossoming of a flower is so beautiful. Similarly the human condition must be accepted for what it is; we must have the courage to mature to the full and learn to come to terms with our own death.[18]

Lena's reaction was an intense emotional one (the "shock" advocated by existential analysts) which recognized the therapist's willingness to participate in her adolescent conflicts and helped to convince her that they could be overcome. After twenty-seven sessions she abandoned her anorexia, which had persisted for three years. It is no coincidence, I think, that flowers and fruit, fruition and decay, were involved in my own recovery: I suspect that I should have responded as Lena did to a similar sort of statement. Not all anorexics are alike, but there is enough similarity among us for me to suspect in addition that in this particular case Selvini Palazzoli came to the root of anorexia nervosa as an existential problem. From my own experience I feel that this is what the anorexic wants to be told or needs to have confirmed: that she is part of nature, and therefore at one with her own body. The body, which includes the mind, is what it is and does what it does; neither its physical characteristics nor its functionings can be divided into the "acceptable" and the "unacceptable," but should be seen as a necessary unity, made up of mutually reinforcing parts. It is what she knows unconsciously but cannot feel; it is what she has lost.

Hilde Bruch does not mention existential analysis as such but, in abandoning a psychoanalytical approach based on causation, she eventually rejects the *why* in favor of the *what* in understanding and treating anorexia nervosa. She has found that her anorexic patients begin to change and improve "under a fact-finding, non-interpretative approach." Such an approach involves a close collaboration between the anorexic and the therapist, who actually listens to what the patient has to say, "paying minute attention to the discrepancies in a patient's recall of his past and to the way he misperceived or misinterpreted current events and often interpreted them in an inappropriate way." Then it is possible to explore alternative perceptions and interpretations with the patient, who can feel that she is actively contributing to the therapy instead of merely being its recipient or even victim. In examining her own development in this way she can come to the realization that her own desires and impulses count, have some weight, and can learn to rely upon her own thoughts and feelings. "Clarification of what the patient is saying," Bruch suggests, "is best carried out in a manner that can be followed by himself, rather than by giving summarizing explanations."

It is important that the therapist talk in simple terms and avoid the use of professional jargon. And it is important that whatever is uncovered or interpreted should be done by the patient herself: she should "say it first," and then the therapist can either agree or disagree as she/he thinks fit. Bruch calls this fact-finding treatment "the constructive use of ignorance," implying that patient and therapist are working together like a couple of scientists in order to unearth facts and unknown factors. "The therapeutic goal," says Bruch, "is to make it possible for the patient to uncover *his* own abilities, *his* resources and inner capacities for thinking, judging and feeling."[19] In the terminology of existential analysis, it is to help the patient find her/his own being-in-the-world. As far as anorexia nervosa is concerned, this seems to me the soundest approach, whether or not drugs or other forms of therapy are involved as well. Anorexics are people who cannot come to terms (for whatever reasons) either with themselves or with the world as they perceive them both. What is needed is realistic self-appraisal: the anorexic must learn to live in the world and with herself, which amounts to the same thing, and includes an acceptance of herself-as-anorexic.

Another more recent development in the treatment of anorexia nervosa is the emergence of self-help groups. There is now an organization called Anorexic Aid, started in 1974, which has a network of "self-care support" groups throughout the UK. [20] In view of the recent popularity of such groups, especially among women, this would seem to be a logical development. As Farber puts it, "group psychology appears at the same time as society erupts with its own solutions for the loss of community, just as the beginnings of psychoanalysis were accompanied by headstrong movements for sexual emancipation." [21] Similarly today, the women's movement is rebelling against the helplessness and dependence of women in general. For this reason alone, self-help groups should be extended some sort of welcome, although it is too early and perhaps impossible—records are not always kept—to talk in terms of success rates. The approach has other advantages, the chief of these being that it rescues the anorexic from her otherwise inevitable isolation, which deepens as the disease progresses. It would have come as a great surprise to me to discover that there were others who felt and thought as I did, let alone others who behaved in the same way; it would also have been a great relief, and it is interesting to note, at this point, that the only person who was of any real help to the anorexic in Katherina Havekamp's novel was another anorexic at the same hospital (see note 2).

Self-help groups, then, fulfill the requirements of friendship, the sharing of experiences in a series of one-to-one relationships which is also at the same time a group relationship. The approach must necessarily be non-interpretative in the professional sense: facts are produced and examined, life histories exchanged. Every story will be different, and it is from these differences, as well as the expected similarities, that the individual anorexic will be able to learn about herself and 'her own unique identity. The groups are run on a non-interfering basis by committed professionals, some of them ex-anorexics themselves, and seem to have a distinct feminist bias.

There is no doubt that this bias provides a helpful way of looking at anorexia nervosa in general terms. But, for various reasons, I do doubt the wisdom of making feminism the ruling ideology in either the understanding or the treatment of anorexics. First, any approach which claims to have found *the* answer to the problem of anorexia nervosa must, by its very nature, be a source of a great many half-truths. For instance,

We believe that the problems anorexic women have in accepting their bodies are merely extreme manifestations of the difficulties of "normal" women. . . . An important part of therapy therefore is the exposing and acknowledging of these internal perceptions and if there is any relationship between the body image of anorexics and normal women—and we believe there is—then we are dealing with a problem which has its roots in the consciousness of all women. [22]

This may well be so, despite the fact that the incidence of anorexia nervosa is also rising in the male population, and despite my own feeling that the relationship between the perceptions of "normal" women and those of anorexics is not quite so straightforward as these writers seem to suppose. However, I can see how the beliefs they express could be of some comfort to the anorexic: half-truths are usually more comforting than whole truths. Whether or not they are more conducive to recovery is another matter. Second, although the self-help method attempts to answer one of the questions left unexplained by family therapy, "why the female body?", it leaves unanswered the other equally important question, "why this particular individual?" In other words, I find that, although individual counseling is given, there is a certain anti-individualistic bias in this approach, of the "I'm OK, you're OK" variety. All I can say in answer to that is that we are not all equally OK: and never will be. But I understand that these groups vary considerably, both as to their methods and their general attitudes, and so my objections may be based on a statement of theory rather than what is actually going on in practice.

Third, the writers of the manifesto quoted above insist that it is essential for anorexics "not to be seen solely as targets for therapy." Anorexics may see themselves as targets, and it is of course laudable that their counselors should be able to identify with them in this experience, but I think a little more objectivity is needed here. Asking the anorexic to take upon herself the burden of a large social problem—the fact that the society in which she lives is geared to the subordination of women—may be analogous to asking her to take upon herself the whole apparatus of Freudian psychodynamics. Many women who are not anorexic can be reduced to hopelessness and helplessness when faced with the recognition of their own status. Like psychoanalysis, an exclusively or aggressively feminist bias may be offering the anorexic too much too soon. When she is in the grip of the disease, she doesn't need theory or ideology, but plain simple facts which can lead her to an *acceptance* of her being-in-the-world rather than reinforce her belief that she and the world are somehow "wrong," or at cross-purposes. Self-help groups, therefore, are more likely to prove effective for the anorexic who is already on the way to recovery, that is, the anorexic who is voluntarily seeking help and already wishes to understand and to overcome her condition.

It has taken me over twenty years to come to terms with the plainer and simpler facts of my own case, let alone the more complex theorizing about anorexia nervosa. My own recovery was preceded, not by drugs or hospitalization, not by family or group therapy, and not by psychoanalysis, but by an intense emotional reaction similar to that experienced by Selvini Palazzoli's patient, Lena. And so it would seem that I am leaning towards what could loosely be called existential therapy as the best form of treatment for anorexics. This is indeed my particular bias, and a reading of Hilde Bruch's work has led me to believe that it is not an entirely subjective one. But, in advocating any sort of treatment, the circumstances of the particular anorexic have to be taken into account: her age, the stage her illness has reached, the length of her illness, her family and social situation, and so on. Some one form of treatment may be more effective in helping one anorexic rather than another. But every form of treatment has its limitations. I have deliberately referred with caution to my recovery rather than my cure. I am not cured, in any real sense, and I doubt if there are many anorexics who would claim otherwise for themselves, whether they have received treatment or not. I don't usually go around looking like a skeleton, but I have had two minor relapses to date. In addition, certain patterns in eating, thinking and feeling remain, which can only be described as anorexic.

7

PROGNOSIS

Opinions as to prognosis vary widely, some people who have worked with anorexics claiming consistently high rates of success, and others expressing doubts as to whether anorexia nervosa is in fact a "curable" disease. Dally[1] suggests that the medical profession is in general more optimistic than the psychiatric because doctors tend to see anorexics at a less advanced stage than do psychiatrists, to whom only the most severe cases are referred. I would add that if anorexia nervosa is seen as a purely medical problem, then of course the disappearance of organic symptoms will be regarded as a "cure." A doctor without psychiatric training, who sees a patient put on weight and hears her claim that she is eating normally, is likely to believe that his task has been accomplished. But anyone who has talked to anorexics about their emotional problems, and who has observed their behavior over long periods, is less likely to take such a sanguine view. Selvini Palazzoli admits that she "cannot share the prognostic optimism expressed by some writers, or accept the high percentages of recoveries they claim."[2] In her view, the false optimism arises from two main causes: first, that many of the patients cited are not suffering from true anorexia nervosa; and, second, that most studies which claim high rates of cure are characterized by the lack of adequate follow-ups, which must be long-term. Her own case histories, she concludes, "show that anorexia nervosa is a grave illness from which patients rarely if ever recover spontaneously." With certain reservations, I am inclined to agree with this conclusion.

It all depends on what is meant by recovery. If it is defined as the ability to function more or less normally, even if in a rather eccentric manner, then there are many anorexics or ex-anorexics at large who have recovered in the sense that they have learned to live with their problems, including that of the disease itself. Perhaps this is as much as anyone can expect. As Sartre has put it, "you can get rid of a neurosis, but you are never cured of yourself."[3] Neither, I would add, can you necessarily be "cured" of your family or of the social milieu out of which that family has evolved. Anorexia nervosa crystalizes in a woman's relationship with her own body, that is, it is based on attitudes which are formed early in life and which social pressures do little if anything to alleviate. The relationship is a fundamental, ever-present one, and I believe it can only rarely be changed permanently by any form of therapeutic intervention. In this sense, full recovery is practically impossible.

The generally accepted criteria for assessing improvement and eventual recovery are the five laid down by Dally and enumerated by him in his monograph, published in 1969. The first is, obviously enough, a substantial weight gain. In his own study of 140 female patients Dally found that 69 percent made a good recovery in terms of body weight, most of them within three years of the onset of the disease, but that, even among these patients, disturbances in eating patterns remained and about a quarter became compulsive eaters. Four of his patients died; the rest remained thin and had been in treatment for years.[4] Bruch reports similar findings. In her study of 45 female patients, completed in 1971, she considered that 23 had made some sort of recovery, although 10 of these were by no means fully cured; 3 died, 1 became obese, and the rest either remained anorexic or were in psychiatric hospitals, or both.[5] Selvini Palazzoli, reporting on 22 patients, found that 9 were chronic and resistant anorexics, while the remaining 13 were relatively recent cases. Of the 9, 3 recovered; 2 were anorexic and mentally disturbed for 10–13 years and then died; 1 became schizophrenic; and 3 improved while still retaining some symptoms of the disease. Of the 13 more recent cases, 9 patients made some sort of recovery, 2 showed marked mental disturbances and a tendency towards bouts of compulsive eating, while the remaining 2 chose to terminate treatment.[6] The depressing statistics which emerge from these and other long-term studies would seem to confirm Selvini Palazzoli and also Bruch's suspicion that Bleuler's dictum, originally applied to schizophrenia, may also be true of anorexia nervosa: "the more exact the follow-up, the rarer a recovery."

When I think about my own weight, which I prefer not to, but often find myself doing obsessively, I have to recognize that it fluctuates within a range of about 20 pounds. The range is not excessive, but I think it indicates that I am still waging some sort of war with my own body. The fluctuations are rapid and geared to my psychological state, while influencing it at the same time. My usual (and, to me, ideal) weight is slightly below normal for a woman of my age and height, but I have great difficulty in maintaining it—in either direction. I still feel that if I "give in" and eat like other people, I shall quickly reached the dreaded weight of 112 pounds—a figure of almost magical significance, after which my weight will shoot up and up, quite beyond my control. In fact, no such thing has ever happened, except of course when I was pregnant, and then it didn't worry me at all. However, when I do reach the dreaded weight, or find myself approaching it, I become depressed and alarmed out of all proportion to the stimulus. I know by now that my response is inappropriate, especially as the weight gain seems repulsive (or, in some cases, even obvious) to no one but myself, and so over the years I have learned to temper it. But my initial reaction is always the same: horror. I have had to ask myself why it is that I still loathe the idea of fatness. My answer has been that when I am fat (as I see it) I simply do not feel myself. I associate fatness in myself, though not in other people, with heaviness, that is, a heaviness of both body and mind which slows me up, making me dull-witted, un-selfconfident and, above all, less able to think for myself. At the same time I know very well that, whatever the nature of these associations, they are based on a false premise. I know that outside factors contribute as much, if not more, than does my body weight to my perception of myself.

The pressures pushing me towards this attitude to fatness are not the immediate social ones from advertising, the media, and allied industries which connect slimness with sexual attractiveness, eternal youth, the ability to wear beautiful clothes, and the confidence to take them off again without embarrassment. On the contrary, I find the prevalent emphasis on youth and slimness at best irritating, and at worst downright insulting to women in general: it tells us that we are only (or chiefly) bodies, and this is precisely what an anorexic cannot accept. For me, the pressures against fatness come from within myself, and arise out of the circumstances of my past life. To be fat is to retreat, not only into my own past but that of my immediate family and the whole network of family relations with both the living and the dead. I was swallowed up in this network, while at the same time being fattened up for the kill. When I was 13, the swallowing family spat me out, but the school continued the fattening process, grooming me for a solid academic career. (The terms "cramming" and "university fodder," common in educational parlance at the time, may help to clarify my metaphor.) The process seemed inexorable and the cycle of being swallowed, spat out (rejected), fattened up, and swallowed again, unbreakable. It is not one conducive to autonomy. If I am fat, as defined above, I run the risk of being devoured—by other people, or by the society in which we all exist. If I am devoured, I shall lose myself, perhaps only to be rejected in return for my self-surrender. If I lose myself, I shall not be able to function. The reasoning behind this argument may seem tortuous, perhaps even incredible, but it makes its own peculiar sense, and can be traced directly to the adolescent conflicts in which I was enmeshed at the onset of my anorexia nervosa.

Similarly, my attitude to thinness has not changed fundamentally, although it has been considerably modified. Fat is still ugly but thin, being asexual, is no longer necessarily beautiful. When I lose weight rapidly, it is always without making any conscious attempt to do so; what I am doing is either consciously maintaining an equilibrium of slimness or not noticing that I have somehow been distracted from eating. Nevertheless, I tend to feel pleased with myself rather than alarmed; at once I feel happier, more self-confident, more independent. Thus far, any conscientious weight-watcher might agree with me. But I can't behave like a conscientious weight-watcher, thinking in terms of calories and weighing every morsel I eat. I'd rebel against any such discipline, probably because it wouldn't be self-imposed. Once I start losing weight, I tend to go on losing weight, until I stop eating altogether for up to three consecutive days. During such periods I find myself lapsing back into some of my old anorexic attitudes: I become acutely aware of other people's shapes and sizes, and feel faintly annoyed if I meet someone thinner than myself; I cook elaborate meals, of which I eat little or nothing; hyperactivity, especially in relation to trivial domestic matters, sets in; and I find myself talking incessantly or dreaming about food.

But three days of starvation are usually enough to make me realize what is happening to me. Nowadays I can admit to myself that I am tired, sleepless, depressed, unable to concentrate, and I force myself to eat—preferably something really fattening like chocolate bars, which I would otherwise avoid on principle. Between these two extremes (which, objectively speaking, are not extremes at all) other anorexia-based traits remain. I can't eat proper meals, that is, I can't eat large amounts of food at any one time, although I can quite happily eat small amounts throughout any one day, even if I feel only slightly hungry. And I don't like people who have no knowledge of my anorexic background (the others are more tactful) to watch me eating and remark on how little I eat.

Apart from the time when I was pregnant or a nursing mother, and apart from my two relapses, my eating habits and attitudes have remained as just outlined for the past twenty years or so. They are clearly still disordered. Although according to Dally's first criterion —that of weight gain or stabilization—I should probably be classified as a "cured" anorexic, I think it would be more accurate to describe myself as a "controlled" or "residual" anorexic. Of course weight gain has to be the primary criterion for improvement or recovery, but my own experience leads me to wonder how many of the patients included in these various surveys and who have gained weight, are in fact maintaining eating patterns, to say nothing of underlying attitudes, similar to mine, despite an appearance of comparative normality. It also reinforces the theory that weight loss in itself is only a small part of the problem.

Dally's second criterion is the resumption of menstruation, and it seems to be generally agreed that this is likely to happen once the patient has reached around 75 percent of her pre-anorexic weight. And so, except in rare cases, it is only those who remain chronically anorexic who continue to be amenorrhoeic. There is some doubt as to whether amenorrhoea in anorexia nervosa is a purely organic symptom of a psychologically based disease. Some writers, such as Bruch, have found that amenorrhoea follows weight loss, and that it is a symptom of starvation. Others, including Dally, maintain that amenorrhoea is due to "emotional influences acting through the hypothalamus," and precedes noticeable weight loss.

This has not been my experience. Although it is well-known that women who lead irregular lives, like air hostesses, and those who are under severe emotional stress, are subject to menstrual irregularities, including amenorrhoea, I am inclined to regard it as an organic symptom. Studies of menstruation in times of war and famine show a clear correlation between amenorrhoea and malnutrition.[7] But at least two of these studies, based on the experiences of women interned in the concentration camps Theresianstadt and Auschwitz, reveal that after 18–20 months, nearly all of the women who had ceased to menstruate (54 percent at Theresianstadt) and had survived, started again. This was not because conditions in the camps had improved—they had, if anything, deteriorated—but because the body had adapted itself to the deprived living standards. Of course the adaptation could also have been a psychological one: in such cases it is impossible to separate the two, because the will to survive may have been an important factor and one which is much too nebulous to define.

But the anorexic insists upon just such a split between her self and her body. She may feel all-powerful in that she has stopped herself from menstruating, and I don't rule out the possibility that in some cases she may be able to do so. Indeed, this was one of the accusations leveled against witches in the Middle Ages—that they were able to control their own menstruation.[8] But it is probably far more common, as well as more likely, that the body, in its own bid for survival, will strike back, adapt, and defeat the psyche, however determined the latter may be. Defeat was certainly my main feeling on the resumption of menstruation, although it didn't fill me with the same horror as before. I accepted it wearily, like the rest of my life, as part of the inevitable. And I have never been able to regard it as anything other than a nuisance and a source of depression. Years later, when I was offered the opportunity to use a contraceptive pill which ensured that I didn't menstruate, I accepted readily and with some relief. The easy resumption of menstruation on the part of the anorexic does not necessarily mean that the phenomenon is a welcome one. Again, the removal of a physical symptom may not correspond to an underlying change in attitude.

Dally's third criterion, the psychosexual development of the patient, is, as he admits, not easy to assess. Weight, menstruation and other organic factors can be measured and quantified, but for anything as difficult to define, let alone assess, as psychosexual development, long follow-ups must be necessary. The simplest measure, Dally suggests, is that of the patient's marital status, and whether or not she has any children. On the face of it, this may seem far too simple and minimal, but the statistics show that marriage and motherhood are comparatively rare among anorexics and ex-anorexics. For instance, Dally's own study cites 38 percent of those whom he considered recovered as having married. The actual figure was 33 patients, 18 of whom had been pregnant at least once; 4 considered their marriages to have failed, and 11 disliked sex. Of Bruch's 45 patients, only 7 married; and Selvini Palazzoli found that, after a five-year follow-up, most of her recovered patients had no wish to marry, to engage in sexual activity, or to take any sort of work outside the home. This seems to be the general picture: only a minority of anorexics, even those who have apparently recovered, lead "normal" sexual lives, the main problem being a reluctance to participate in sexual acts.

Selvini Palazzoli suggests that anorexia nervosa involves an "ambivalent homosexual dependence on the mother." If this were so, we might expect a large proportion of anorexics to be homosexual or to become actively so after recovery. But, to the surprise of some writers, nothing of the sort happens. It doesn't surprise me. The anorexic's immediate quarrel is with her own body, the female body, which at the height of the disease is a loathed and even repulsive object. It is hardly likely that in later life it will become an object of erotic desire or satisfaction. And so the general picture for the majority of girls who have been anorexic remains, in their womanhood, one of asexuality combined with an aversion to childbirth.

Being one of the few who have married and have had children, I find this picture depressing and the figures which constitute it surprisingly high. It is not that I hold any particular brief for marriage, as such, but I have already stressed how important personal relationships, especially the one-to-one relationship, are to the anorexic. If the one special person in her life—whom she needs—remains her mother or a mother-substitute, then no growth has been achieved. Many anorexics solve this problem by entering into asexual marriages where the husband can take the mother's place and the wife remain a little girl. But I think most of us would agree that a life of celibacy, founded upon an aversion to sex rather than a freer choice, is one in which there is a great deal missing. Of course, many women who have never been anorexic choose not to have children. They have their reasons, some more rational than others. The anorexic has her reasons too: they are based on a fear and horror of the workings of the female body. She is still refusing to see herself as part of the natural world, and as long as she continues this refusal, she will remain temperamentally anorexic, whatever her eating habits. In contrast to the majority of anorexics, I always assumed, on some unconscious level, that one day, when I was ready, I should marry and have children—just like everyone else. Psychosexual conflicts are not necessarily the only or the primary ones at the root of anorexia nervosa, but in cases where they are, it would seem that they are the most difficult to resolve.

Dally's fourth criterion is the degree of independence shown by patients who have regained more or less normal weight. This again is difficult to assess. Leaving home, going abroad, and so on, may be good prognostic signs in the short term, but in my opinion they do not necessarily point to any surety for permanent recovery. In themselves such moves could merely be evidence of the same undirected or misdirected need for autonomy which chacterizes anorexia nervosa. Before they can be used as criteria for recovery, we need to know how successful and how permanent such moves are. It is possible that they could lead to loneliness, isolation and the secret pursuit of an anorexic life in the absence of any close kind of scrutiny. More cogently, Dally and others have found that a significant proportion of recovered anorexics—in his experience, nearly a quarter—take up teaching, medicine or allied work; that is, they enter what are known as the "caring professions." As I see it, such professions have the following advantages to offer the anorexic: they provide an opportunity for dedication to work and devotion to others without having to entail uncomfortably close and therefore threatening relationships; they offer a degree of independence combined with a dependence on either a particular institution or a particular set of professional rules; they are hierarchical structures in which the individual's position is clearly defined, both in relation to her colleagues and to those in her care. The crux of the matter is that in these professions the anorexic can maintain her ambivalent attitude to other people: she can work within the recognized boundaries of a pseudo-family without having to become involved in the intense personal conflicts which have characterized her own family life.

Despite an intermittently recurring fantasy of becoming a psychoanalyst, I have not entered the "caring professions," and feel no real attraction towards them. When I was ten-years-old my father told me that I was going to be a writer (having presumably changed his mind about the Prime Ministership). He gave me an exercise book, which I still have, and told me to start practicing by keeping a diary. "Whatever you do," he added, "don't teach." I have taken his advice on both counts, and so it would seem that I am still doing what my parents, or perhaps only father, wanted me to do. But I am also doing what I want to do. I work at home and alone; but I don't live alone; I can care for others, become involved in their lives, while getting on with my own work. I didn't consciously plan this way of life. It has evolved over the years, but I can see that its evolution has not been entirely unconnected with anorexic preferences, and that it has not been conducive to the abandonment of anorexic attitudes. I married a man who was more than capable of supporting me financially, and I accepted the support unquestioningly instead of thinking about the future and making some attempt to provide for myself. To write may require a certain independence of mind but, because I have never earned a living by writing, I cannot in all honesty describe myself as an independent woman.

Dally's fifth criterion is more difficult yet to access, and is probably even impossible, except perhaps in purely clinical terms. It refers to the mental state of the patient, something which can only be gauged in such seemingly clear diagnoses as to whether she is depressed, disturbed, and so on. Such states of mind are often a matter of subjective judgment on the part of the clinician and impossible for the patient herself to define. I shall not attempt to describe my state of mind, except to say that it is, like most other people's, variable. To return to Selvini Palazzoli's point, such assessments can only be made on the basis of long-term and, in my opinion, consistently frequent follow-ups. Minuchin and his colleagues state that in their studies the follow-up periods ranged from one and a half to seven years. And they claim a recovery rate, both physical and social, of 86 percent. But the table actually given in their book shows that only 1 case out of 53 was followed up for or after seven years. Apart from this one, the longest follow-up period given is four years nine months, and the norm two to three years. Their claim to such a high recovery rate begins to look very doubtful. [9]

The question arises: how long is a long-term follow-up? It is one which Minuchin *et al.* are themselves aware of, and indeed they criticize other studies for having given insufficient attention, or none at all, to the matter. I would agree with them, but would add that two to three years is a totally inadequate period upon which to base an assessment of permanent recovery; five years is slightly less so; but even seven is not long enough. If I had been followed up by Minuchin and his colleagues after seven years, they would have found a "normal" if rather harassed housewife with two small children and exhibiting none of the hallmarks of anorexia nervosa. Even without the benefit of six months of family therapy, I should have seemed to have recovered completely. Coping with two small children (mine are fourteen months apart in age) is a full-time, all-demanding occupation. I had no time to think about my own body when there were other bodies which needed my constant care. I scarcely had time to think about myself at all. But if I had been followed up three to four years later, I should have presented a very different picture. In my opinion, the absolute minimum follow-up term is 10 years; 20 years would provide a more realistic assessment, and 30 years would be better still. I base this opinion not only on my own experience, but on the supposition that a woman who has once been anorexic is most likely to relapse when she finds herself placed in a situation similar to the one in which she found herself immediately before the onset of her teenage anorexia. It cannot be predicted when such situations are likely to recur. And they in turn point to a situation in which conflicts from further back in her past re-emerge and have to be re-enacted.

My first relapse occurred 10–11 years after my teenage anorexia had come to an end. The circumstances of the relapse may be extreme, but they are not unique, being what a friend of mine refers to as "the Mrs. Famous Syndrome." It happened in the mid-1960s when the British pop music boom was at its height. I was married to a pop star, a man whose face was so well-known that it was impossible for him to walk down the main street of any town in the UK without being recognized and mobbed by teenage girls. In fact, it was impossible for us to go anywhere in public without being pestered by people, either directly and demandingly, or indirectly by means of concentrated staring and conversations (not always complimentary) which could easily be overheard by us. The general public seems to assume that fame renders a person deaf as well as blind and automatically deprives him of his right to privacy. This may be the price of fame for the person himself, and I'm sure there are many people who are willing to pay it. But for his wife it is an undue exaction, like having to pay taxes on money which one has never earned and enjoyed. Everywhere we went, my husband was feted, wooed, extravagantly praised. Apart from the times when I was actually physically attacked or subject to abusive and obscene phone calls, I was ignored. Meanwhile, there was a woman to clean the house, a nanny to look after the children, and the band's roadie to act as chauffeur. Sometimes my husband was away from home for long periods, and so I hardly saw or talked to him. Sometimes I went with him, and so I hardly saw or talked to my children. If I was with him, I couldn't be with them, and vice versa. If I stayed at home, I was lonely and depressed. If I went away with my husband, I found myself in a situation in which there was little privacy and I had no real function. There was no real function for me anywhere. I was nothing; I was nowhere. I had become a thing again, a thing living or half-living in a world of unreality.

The obvious question to ask is, why on earth did I allow myself to be placed in such a position? I could answer: because it all happened so quickly that I didn't know what was going on. Or: because I didn't know what else to do. The latter comes closer to the truth and is, as I see it, a typically anorexic one. I felt that there was no escape, and that somehow I was to blame for my feelings of uselessness and depression. I even went to see my GP, who prescribed a course of anti-depressants, which I continued to take for the next seven years. But I did try to fight back, to establish and maintain my identity in my own inadequate way. I started to write reviews and then a novel, in which I hoped to set out my own wry view of the madness in which our lives seemed to be enveloped. But writing novels is a slow and arduous business in which the rewards are few and the results slow to be seen. By contrast, the pop business moves (or moved then) at breakneck speed, its rewards immediately visible. I had little confidence in what I was doing. And I was losing weight. At first no one noticed, not even myself. During the 1960s it was fashionable not only to be slim, but to be extraordinarily thin. The Duchess of Windsor's remark that one can never be too rich or too thin was widely quoted, and to me it sums up the whole period. Once I realized how thin I was, and others began to compliment me on my appearance, I began to spend a lot of money on clothes and to take an extravagant interest in my own body. At expensive restaurants I would pick at my food, drink a lot, talk a lot, and then move on to some club, staying up until the small hours. During the day I wrote. I had become hyperactive.

Once I reached this stage I became determined to stay thin, determined in fact to be thinner than anyone else: this was one game at which no one could beat me. Becoming thin had roused me from my inertia and, once again, had helped to dispel feelings of hopelessness and helplessness. Soon I was living on vitamin pills and white wine and eating only at weekends. Then even that became too much: weekend eating was followed by purging or often omitted altogether. Meanwhile I was regularly giving dinner parties, over which I took great pains, for up to 12 people at a time. My novel was accepted for publication, and I immediately started on another one—the one about the girl in the glass coffin. I convinced myself that I was happy. Hyperactivity continued but soon, despite the pills, depression began to assert itself, and I had to drive myself to do anything at all. Even when I started to fall asleep at my desk, even when I became amenorrhoeic, even when the tiniest clothes from my favorite shops were all obviously too big for me and I weighed just over 84 pounds, I still couldn't admit to myself what was happening, and that I was in fact anorexic, as I had been before.

I think what saved me from this relapse was the publication of my first novel—an event which coincided with the completion of the second one. All of a sudden I was Sheila MacLeod again instead of just Mrs. Paul Jones. Sheila MacLeod was a person who had been lost, buried, for years, and I found to my intense surprise that she was still alive. A newspaper interview at the time described me as frail, pale, wispy, inclined to shiver even when the sun was out, and looking ten years younger than my actual age. The description surprised me: it was that of a skinny, ailing, eighteen-year-old. It was too, of course, that of an anorexic.

When it was picked up by a reviewer (whom I had never met) I was even more surprised: she expressed her contempt for frail, pale women living in Islington with rich husbands, implying that such people had no business to be writing novels, and were not to be taken seriously. In some strange way the interview and the review combined to make me realize what their writers had obviously not: how unhappy I actually was. My existence was being acknowledged in public, but my physical appearance was also being commented on as if it were of some relevance and something remarkable, whereas to me it was perfectly acceptable and none of anyone's business but my own. I was puzzled, as if an important fact had somehow escaped me, but I still couldn't/ wouldn't admit that I was anorexic. But, in general, what publication did for me-as-anorexic was to make me realize how withdrawn I had become, and how remote from other people, shut up as I was in my own room, and in my own mind, even when I was appearing in public as Mrs. Famous and playing a role I should never have chosen for myself. In order to be myself, I had isolated myself, and in doing so I had lost myself, or a large part of myself. But at the same time I had found myself—another, perhaps larger, part of myself. This much I understood at the time, but I never made any but the vaguest connection between my mental and physical states. However, it was then that I started gradually, very gradually, to eat again.

During my second relapse I was much more aware of what was happening to me, although I felt no more capable of controlling it. It occurred seven years after the end of my second anorexic phase (which lasted approximately two years) and shortly after my mother died. She had been ill for about a year, and the cause of her death was cancer of the breast—which is, I think, of some significance in relation both to my previous history and my subsequent behavior. I was not emotionally close to my mother, saw her rarely, knew that she was going to die, and yet her death came as a tremendous shock to me. All this is normal enough, but in my case the period of grief and mourning continued long after what is recognized to be the normal limit (about a year) and took its own peculiar form. When someone dies, the bereaved person goes through a series of emotional reactions: shock, grief, guilt, anger both with the dead person and with those who might have been able to prevent her death, and a new awareness of her/his own mortality. I went through all those phases, but at the same time my behavior reverted, though in a slightly different form from the previous times, to that of an anorexic.

I probably started to lose weight immediately after her death, but in such circumstances weight loss is not unusual. Certainly anyone who commented on my appearance attributed the change to grief, and of course they were right. It was not until three or four months later that I developed a positive aversion to eating: as soon as the food was in my mouth I felt the urge to spit it out again. Somehow it would have been wrong to swallow it. If I forced myself to swallow it, it felt wrong, morally as well as physically, to have it in my body, and I started once more on the purging routine. Meanwhile, I had become hyperactive, leading a more than usually full social life, and taking an excessive interest in clothes and my general appearance. I also started determinedly on another novel, having published nothing for three to four years. Again, I cooked a lot; again, I did everything I could to avoid eating.

By the summer, three months later, I had become amenorrhoeic, my weight having dropped to below 98 pounds. And it was to go on dropping. I had been depressed enough throughout the preceding months, but at about that time something happened to precipitate me into a state where I simply couldn't stop crying. My father asked me to sort out my mother's clothes, delivering the wearable ones to the local Oxfam shop, and throwing the rest away. (This involved a special trip to Wales.) I was reluctant, but I agreed because I knew he couldn't bear to do it himself. Reluctant as I was, though, I wasn't prepared for the horror involved in the task. I felt it was my mother I was throwing away, and the sight of garment after garment stained in the same place made me want to scream. For weeks afterwards I was inconsolable, my defenses completely eroded. Then, one day, I found myself so weak that my legs had become paralyzed and I couldn't walk upstairs. The doctor was called and could find nothing wrong with me, apart from the fact that I was obviously underweight. He prescribed tranquilizers, and I could walk again. A few days later I remembered my mother having said, the last time I saw her, "I sleep down here these days because my legs won't carry me upstairs."

It was shockingly clear to me that I had been identifying with my mother—shocking because I thought I knew more about myself and about the rudiments of Freudian psychoanalysis than to behave in such a conventionally hysterical manner. One of the perpetual mysteries of individual human behavior is that knowledge, as opposed to experience, so rarely changes it. It was only when I could tell myself, "you are not your mother," and believe myself, that I could see the meaning of my anorexic state. "All authorities are agreed," says Selvini Palazzoli, "that the child's original experience with the primary object is a corporeal—incorporative one."[10] In other words the original relationship with the mother is characterized by an identification in which the mother's body is seen as an extension of the child's. My second relapse would seem to bear out this assertion, and points to the possibility that the primary experience of introjection/projection had never been properly resolved. I had identified with my mother to such an extent that I took her symptoms and, by implication, her death, upon myself. In becoming anorexic at this time, I was saying (at least) three things. The first was: "I want to be free of you, mother, but I feel guilty about such disloyalty, and so I can't free myself altogether." The second was:

"If I am I, I'm alive; if I am you, I'm dead, and I can't tell the difference." The third was: "I've got to be me (the anorexic) because I don't want to die." It seems to me that my second relapse shows a clear-cut case of anorexia nervosa as a bid, against all odds, for both autonomy and life.

Despite their apparent dissimilarities, the two relapses have certain features in common. Both involve the loss of a loved object, the first through separation and alienation (from my husband) and the second through death (of my mother). At the same time both involve the inability to break away from a loved object by whom one is swallowed up to such an extent that the boundaries between it and oneself become indistinct. I often think that if there is a predisposition to anorexia nervosa, it is the psychological equivalent of a severe deficiency in the immune system: people who suffer from such deficiencies do not reject skin grafts or viruses and/or bacteria because the body is incapable of distinguishing between what is self and what is not-self. During the first relapse I was nothing but an extension of my husband and his career; during the second I was the living extension of a dead person, a surrogate for her. And yet, resenting them both for their apparent desertion of me, I needed desperately to be myself alone (whatever that was) and a part of neither of the other people. Anorexia nervosa had been my strategy, my only weapon, in the past, and when the need arose I used it again.

Other people may have acted differently in similar situations but, having been anorexic before, I "chose" the reaction which I assumed to be foolproof and which I believed to embody my own peculiar talent: that of starving myself. The initial choice was an unconscious one, but the justifications which followed it were both conscious and determined. And of course they were secret. And of course I was untruthful, never saying to others, "I won't eat," but always, "I can't eat." Even now when I know something about the reasons for my having been anorexic, and when I know intellectually that self-starvation is ultimately a futile process, I cannot say with any certainty that I shall never become anorexic again. Anorexia nervosa is still *my* neurosis. And, although I no longer have a mother or a rich husband to trigger it off for me, I know that it is always there to be used as a last resort and a final act of defiance against the too-closely-impinging world which may threaten to engulf or annihilate me. I suspect that there are many anorexics and ex-anorexics who, if they were honest with themselves, would admit to feeling the same.

When we turn from individual prognosis to that of the disease in general terms of prevalence and growth, there is scarcely more reason for optimism. During 1972–5 (a period which included follow-ups) Crisp, Kalucy and Palmer studied two comprehensive schools, and seven from the independent sector,* in order to find out the prevalence of anorexia nervosa.[11] In the comprehensive schools the incidence was comparatively low, but higher in the all-girls' school than in the mixed one. The incidence in independent schools was noticeably higher, especially among girls aged 16 or over. It is interesting to note that in the course of the survey two of the original nine independent schools "were advised by their Parents' Association or Board of Governors to proceed no further." This sort of defensiveness, so typical of such schools, is not only unhelpful, but in itself revealing: misfits must not be paraded in public, although (and perhaps because) the self-righteous and unimaginatively conformist attitudes prevailing in such places may have helped to create the misfits in the first place. In the remaining 7 schools a total of 27 cases was identified, and the overall prevalence amounted to approximately 1 girl in every 200. For those under the age of 16, this amounted to 1.7 per 1000, and for those over 16, 10.5 per 1000, or approximately one in every 100. Such girls are likely to come from middle-class homes, but "subjects with anorexia nervosa and their families may be advised (mistakenly) that they should go away to boarding school as a form of treatment, irrespective to some extent of social background." I should heavily endorse that "mistakenly." The authors of this paper conclude that, "the disorder is by no means confined to middle-class families, as our out-patient experience shows, but the association is a strong one."

The evidence, corroborated by other studies, is that anorexia nervosa is not only increasing, but beginning to spread itself throughout the population, regardless of social class. It is also more prevalent in higher

*Comprehensive schools are roughly equivalent to American public schools; independent schools correspond to private schools.

age groups than it has been in the past. The authors of the prevalence study quoted above suggest, "It is our impression that the disorder is even more common amongst university undergraduates and others of like age." Their impression is borne out by a paper published in 1973 by May Duddle, who studied patients referred to the student Health Center at Manchester University during the period 1966–72.[12] All 23 patients were diagnosed according to Dally's criteria, and were born in the years 1949–53. The figures recorded at the Health Center show that in 1966 and 1967, no students were referred for treatment for anorexia nervosa; in 1968, there was one case, in 1969 two, in 1970 seven, and in 1971, thirteen. In contrast to this sharp increase there was no coincidental change in the diagnoses of other psychiatric disorders. Neither could the increase be attributed to the larger proportion of females in the university population, because although the total number of students went up during this period, there was no change in the male/female ratio. Duddle suggests that because all the anorexic students were born soon after the severe food rationing of the Second World War, there could have been a marked increase in the amount of food consumed by both mothers and babies in the following years, and so anorexia nervosa might be linked with sudden unrestricted food intake in early childhood. There may indeed be a link of some sort, but if it is as specific as she suggests, we should expect that by now the prevalence statistics would have somewhat stabilized. There is no evidence that this is so. On the contrary, Crisp and his colleagues (among many others) have shown that prevalence is still on the increase.

Why? The question, however difficult to answer, has to be asked. Perhaps the statistics themselves should be questioned, on two grounds. First, are all the girls and young women included in these various studies actually suffering from true or primary anorexia nervosa? Second, can the increase be attributed to the fact that the disorder has become more "visible," that is, more likely than before to be identified, diagnosed and treated? Even if the answer to the first question is a partial "yes," and to the second a partial "no," it seems to me that the evidence in favor of an overall increase in prevalence is still very solid. It would, I think, be dangerous to assume otherwise. And so, at once, several other questions have to be asked. What is it that working-class girls now have in common with girls from the middle to upper classes which was not previously shared by the two groups? What are the pressures now felt by young women which were previously characteristic of adolescent or pre-adolescent girls? And why is the disease, though on the increase, still mainly confined to females? It must be that feelings of hopelessness and helplessness have become more widespread among adolescent girls and young women, regardless of social class; that the bid for autonomy has become a more pressing need for this same group; and that the female body has become more than ever the focal point at which various conflicts gather and express themselves. The question remains as to why these things should be so.

The apparent disregard for social class as a new factor in anorexia nervosa is not, as some writers have suggested, due to the fact that we live in an increasingly classless society. As far as I am concerned, that is not a fact at all. It may be that, since the introduction of comprehensive schools, we have a more equitable educational system which, in providing opportunities for higher education for larger numbers of schoolchildren, also provides concomitant opportunities for social mobility. And it may be that these latter opportunities occur at college or university rather than at schools. Less able children (which in practice and for social reasons really meant the working class) are no longer segregated in secondary modern schools, having been written off as academic failures at the age of 11, in comparison to grammar-school children. But how equitable is the system in practice? Many schools still stream their classes,* and of course the wealthy can still opt out altogether and into the independent sector. There is a pretense of social equity, just as there is a pretense of equity between boys and girls, and in this latter case, a promise of equity which cannot be fulfilled. Many schools encourage girls to specialize in subjects which have traditionally been the preserve of boys. It may be that this attitude, in itself admirable, can lead to confusion within the teenage girl as to her own role: she may pass her O-levels in physics and technical drawing, but it will be the boy who gets the job. And it is important for her to get a job because she can no longer look on marriage and children as a full-time permanent

*Group students homogeneously.

career. At the same time she has been educated beyond the menial sort of job her mother or other female relatives may have been forced to take in order to supplement the family income. Once she has a few O-levels to her credit, the working-class girl will be less likely to opt for immediate marriage or a job on the assembly line than was her mother. But because unemployment is high, she may have to, or feel that she has to. And a university graduate may find herself in a similar position. In both cases she will feel frustrated and under-used, perhaps even helpless and hopeless.

But all this is speculation. America and Sweden, where anorexia nervosa is also on the increase, have had a more equitable system than ours for many years. It may be that in those countries, as in this one, there is still a discrepancy between educational opportunities and career opportunities. Selvini Palazzoli suggests that marked rises in the incidence of anorexia nervosa coincide with sudden changes in the social position of women. She adds that any such supposition is impossible to verify, and I agree with her, but I do believe that there is, at any given time, a firm link between the disorder and what is expected of women—from any source.

I would hazard that if anorexia nervosa is spreading from the middle to the working class, it is less because class barriers are disappearing than because we all now share a common culture to an unprecedented extent. Before the advent of the electronic media, orthodox culture came from books and required literacy. I am not suggesting that the working classes at this time were illiterate, never read books, or indeed did not possess a strong culture or cultures of their own, but that the dissemination of information—political, historical, literary or artistic— was once largely the prerogative of the middle classes. Now that we are living in what has been called the post-literate age, we can all watch wars in South East Asia or admire the treasures of the Louvre in the comfort of our own living rooms, or wherever we keep our TV sets. Similarly, we are all subject to advertising—from TV, radio, magazines, billboards—whether we like it or not.

In one sense, the world has become smaller as it approaches the global village prophesied by Marshall McLuhan but, in another sense, it has also become larger and more confusing. There is simply too much information too readily available: our attention is being competed for from too many different sources. The messages conflict, and adults are likely to have less difficulty in sorting them out than children or adolescents. For the adolescent girl or young woman the conflicts which concern her most nearly are likely to be those involving her perception of herself. For the anorexic, these conflicts in self-perception will tend to be at their strongest in three different areas: that of herself in relation to adults, especially other women; that of herself in relation to the male world; and that of herself in relation to her own body. The boundaries of these areas overlap, but I have divided them in order to clarify my necessarily speculative arguments.

It is probably true that, as Anorexic Aid and the Anorexia Counselling Service have it in one of their leaflets, the pre-anorexic adolescent feels that "adulthood requires her to become the female stereotype (which, in spite of token equality, still demands emotional and financial dependence, giving without taking, passivity and lack of personal identity)."[13] But there is nothing new in this situation. My point, which the authors of this leaflet only hint at, is that there is now more than one female stereotype, and that it may be impossible for the pre-anorexic to reconcile or to choose among those which are offered. It is notable that in all the studies I have mentioned, most of the mothers of anorexic patients did not do full-time work outside the home, however exceptional such a choice may have been within their own social milieu. Even if this is no longer true, I suspect that the stereotype of the all-succoring mother-figure or "Mum" remains, particularly in working-class homes. But the woman who makes her way in a man's world is another stereotype—and is perhaps exemplified by Mrs. Thatcher. So, too, is the sex symbol, whose private life might have made our mothers blush, but whose activities are now accepted in the media as being not only worthy of our admiration and envy, but tinged at the same time by a certain romantic tragedy. I am not suggesting that such stereotypes have not existed before—just that they are now more in evidence, and that the first, with which the average anorexic has been brought up, tends to be devalued in comparison to the others.

Similarly, magazines aimed specifically at teenagers and young women offer conflicting notions of womanhood. Publications such as

Cosmopolitan may feature women who have had considerable success in their own fields, but the main emphasis is still on how to get your man (or men) and keep him, mainly through sexual wiles. Others, usually for a younger age group, may give realistic advice in answer to real sexual and emotional problems submitted by their readers, while featuring the sort of fiction which evades the central emotional issues of adolescence, and whose eventual outcome is wedding-bells. The adolescent girl is being told that she should be independent, but not to the extent where she is going to antagonize men; that she must make full use of her intellectual resources, but not to the extent where they could interfere with her primary role as wife-and-mother; that she must be sexy and seductive, but still allow the man to take the dominant sexual role, in case she may injure his male pride; and that the pursuit of domestic skills—such as cooking—is necessary not because they can in themselves be creative pursuits, but because they are going to make some man so happy and comfortable that he could never contemplate leaving either her or their home. The advice, never of course expressed *in toto* from any one source, adds up to this: you can go so far, but no further. How on earth anyone is supposed to manage all this, I don't know. And how can the adolescent girl cope with such contradictory pressures? Perhaps the weapon against the helplessness induced by such a demanding total stereotype has, for an increasingly large number of young women, become anorexia nervosa.

In my case, my body seemed to be my only weapon: for girls and young women of today it may seem to be a more obvious and immediate one than it would have seemed then. After all, the advertising industry, as well as certain newspapers and magazines, is obsessed with the female body. It is paraded, like food, as something to be consumed. To any potential anorexic, this is a horrifying presentation, and a fate to be avoided at all costs. In addition, the idea of the perfect female body, as presented by advertisers and others, does not correspond with the actual bodies of most normal women, and depends largely on exaggeration. The women concerned generally have abnormally huge breasts, or else are abnormally tall and slim. The implications are that if you don't have "big tits," you are not "sexy" (that is, not a *real* woman) but, at the same time, if you are not lean and elegant, you are not an expensive, and therefore desirable, object to be coveted and purchased.

In both cases, the female body is being used as live bait: in order to sell newspapers or more expensive consumer goods. The images presented and the ways in which they are used are insulting to women, and make a lot of us angry. But others may be made to feel confused and inferior by them: their own bodies, especially at the lumpy adolescent stage, don't come up to scratch, either as sexy or expensive objects. This could be as depressing as the idea of being consumed is horrifying. Neither idea can be ignored, because we have been conditioned from childhood to regard our bodies as the primary expressions of ourselves in a way in which boys never have been. Boys go in for body-building, sport, and so on, but in such cases the male body is regarded as an active, working thing rather than a passive vehicle intended to provide gratification. The irony of this attitude is that the female body is more "active" than the male because it produces children. It is not a thing to be gazed at and possessed, but a functional organism. All women know this, but perhaps none feels the irony more painfully than the anorexic, to whom the bodily changes which prepare her for childbirth are often only an additional trauma.

What I have been suggesting is that these contradictory stereotypes of womanhood, and in particular the female body, are part of our common culture and not the property of any one social class. I would suggest in addition that the pressures engendered by such stereotypes may be felt more keenly than before among the university population because it is then that young women may be confronted for the first time with seemingly far-reaching choices as to their own future. Women are going to university in increasingly large numbers, and for many this step may represent the first break from home and the immediate family. Then there are academic pressures: a girl who seemed to be of outstanding ability in a provincial or private school may suddenly find herself among her intellectual peers or superiors. To most people, such a change in environment is probably stimulating, but to the anorexic, it is a potentially dangerous situation. She is swallowed up in a large, perhaps impersonal, institution where she must survive without the support of her family and without the self-boosting knowledge that she has the ability (in comparison to others) to carry her through her course. If she is the first woman in her family to attend university, she may feel all the more strongly the pressure to succeed and the concomitant fear of failure.

There may also be social pressures which she has to face for the first time. If she has attended a single-sex school (as do the majority of anorexics) she will find herself in a world which also contains men as colleagues and as possible sexual partners. This latter possibility could be frightening on two counts. First, she may not be able to find herself a "boyfriend" with the ease which seems to be characteristic of most of the other women around her, either because she considers herself to be too unattractive (fat?) or because she has never been trained to take or pursue any initiative as far as men are concerned. Comparing herself with others, her sense of inferiority will increase. Second, her very passivity may lead her to the sort of relationship in which she feels herself to be dominated or "used" sexually by some man, and a further loss of identity will ensue. All this is guesswork, but it is informed guesswork which, when the pieces are fitted together, produces a climate conducive to the growth of anorexia nervosa. There is the artificially isolated community in which, however close-knit it may appear, the individual feels alienated. In it, the atmosphere, both academic and social, will be competitive. For many women, the years at university can provide a moratorium during which the individual can find herself; for the anorexic, bewildered in the present and dreading the future, they could provide the perfect opportunity for losing herself.

Crisp and his colleagues suggest that anorexia nervosa may be far more common than is generally supposed both among women of a similar age who do not attend university, and among those who are beyond the average age of a university population.[14] Their observations are drawn from their own clinical work and that of others, but it is obviously more difficult to come up with reliable figures when dealing with isolated individuals than it is when dealing with large institutions where medical and psychiatric records are kept. Dally refers to a phenomenon known as "anorexia tardive," which affects women between the ages of 31 and 59. They tend to be nervous and voluble, like sparrows, and their marital relationships, he states, are never satisfactory.[15] Kellett, Trimble and Thorley have described a postmenopausal case of anorexia nervosa in which the patient developed all the classic symptoms at the age of 52.[16] They conclude that although anorexia is "predominantly a disease of onset in adolescence, it may be present at any age." It would be interesting to know how many of these older women were "hidden" anorexics (that is, those who like myself received no treatment) in adolescence or early adulthood. If some were, they are living proof of the tenacity of anorexia nervosa; if not, we must conclude that the disorder is spreading itself throughout a much wider age range than has been supposed, as well as throughout a wider class range.

The increase in prevalence is, as most writers agree, general and not confined to what was considered to be the typical age or class. The incidence among males is also rising, although only slightly. I have already implied that the ready access to information, which has undergone a similar spread, has some connection with this phenomenon, but I should like to make it clear that I discount all theories which advance "epidemic slimming," or the emulation of much-publicized thin women, as an explanation for the increase in prevalence. The connection is not that simple. Even in the 1960s, when slimness was at a premium and mass hysteria among teenage girls nothing unusual, there was no marked epidemic of anorexia nervosa, and in fact the rate of prevalence is higher now. There may or may not have been a larger number of skinny teenage girls around then than there are now, but they were not necessarily anorexics.

The anorexia nervosa syndrome is psychopathologically distinct, and by now should be recognizable after a short examination. Slimness can be willed; non-eating can be willed; anorexia nervosa, although it depends on a stupendous act of will, cannot be willed in the same conscious way. Women who have a strong sense of identity and happy relationships with their own bodies will not be susceptible to it. It could be argued that women who are habitual dieters are unhappy with their own bodies, and I would agree with this but add that, for reasons which I have already suggested, the quality of unhappiness is different. Perhaps the difference can be summed up as follows. The dieter or slimmer is saying, "I am unhappy with the way I look, and must do something about it." The anorexic is saying, "I am unhappy with this thing which

I disown and which others call me—my body. I should like to subdue it and keep it in its proper place so that it won't keep pestering me."

Women's groups involved in self-help for anorexics often seem to believe that the problems anorexics have with their bodies are only those of "normal" women writ large, and to a certain extent I would agree, but I must insist again that the difference is qualitative as well as quantitative. In this context, the leaflet prepared for the BBC 2 TV programme, *Grapevine*, is worth looking at.[17] The authors believe, as I do, that,

> Our society encourages women to look on their bodies as objects; to feel that they must conform to externally-imposed ideals and the whims of fashion. This alienates women from their own bodies—and leads some to starve themselves while others overeat in rebellion—and is reflected in the current obsession with food, calories and weight-watching.

So far, so sensible, as applied to women in general. And I would even agree with their following statement that food, for women, seems to have replaced sex as a neurotic focus for guilt. However, the authors go on to say, "Women with anorexia take this to extremes, feeling their worth depends entirely on their body being a certain shape and weight; they split themselves into mind and body, at war with each other. This approach seems to explain why nearly everyone with an eating problem is female." I only wish it did, but there is a jump in the argument. There is a war going on within the anorexic between mind and body, but I can't accept that the precipitating cause of this war is only, or even mainly, a feeling that the size and shape of her body constitutes the measure of her worth. I have tried to show that, in my own case, such considerations were of secondary importance. And, although I am prepared to accept that they may be of more importance to other anorexics than they have been to myself, I don't think that the split between mind and body can be accounted for in terms which pertain in the larger part to the body alone. They must also pertain to the mind, and I have tried to show that they involve problems of introjection and projection, separation and loss, helplessness and hopelessness, lack of identity and autonomy, and that anorexia nervosa is a last stand against being engulfed by such emotional disasters.

8

CONCLUSIONS

It must be concluded that there are certain identifiable predisposing and precipitating factors involved in the making of an anorexic. Predisposition is a term open to misinterpretation because it carries connotations of organic symptoms or characteristics which have been present since early childhood. Despite various suggestions which have been made to the contrary, I think all such connotations should be discounted. For instance, a tendency to be overweight is not in itself a predisposing factor: what counts is the attitude of others—first, parents and other adults, then contemporaries—towards a girl's weight and general physical appearance.

Predisposition is concerned with a girl's early and continuing experience within the family and within a wider social context; it is a matter of long-term attitudes firmly maintained within both contexts. As Dally puts it, "It is apparent that many patients are repeating, in anorexia nervosa, a similar pattern of behaviour which developed during childhood in response to parental pressures. The reaction of patient and parent during these earlier 'rehearsals' will sometimes indicate the likely outcome, and suggest ways in which the patient may be helped."[1] And so the identification of predisposing factors is important in determining both treatment and prognosis for the individual anorexic. It is also important because, in the absence of the predisposing factors, those which are generally considered to precipitate anorexia nervosa would probably not be effective. In short, anorexia nervosa should be seen as evolving from a concatenation of circumstances, both past and present, rather than appearing suddenly and for no sufficiently good reason, as a particular response to a particular stimulus.

At this point it seems appropriate for me to offer up a recipe. Its purpose is not to persuade the anorexic to eat or to encourage her obsessive interest in cooking. It is a recipe not for the use but for the creation of an anorexic, and should provide a banquet, not where she eats but where she is eaten. I hope it will be of particular use to parents, as well as offering some sort of minimal guidance to teachers, doctors, therapists and others who are faced with the resulting concoction. Not all the ingredients (or predisposing factors) are absolutely necessary, and some are more easily available than others, but the general idea is to make use of as many of them as possible: as in all good cooking, improvisation and imagination can play an important or even decisive part. At the same time the two basic principles upon which the success of the recipe depends should be borne in mind. They are the engendering of mystification through a series of contradictory attitudes, especially towards womanhood; and the consistent stifling of all attempts at autonomy on the part of the growing girl. The recipe is not infallible, human beings being unpredictable creatures, but if it is followed with the dedication of a Dr. Frankenstein, there is more than a little hope that results similar to his may be achieved.

1 Social Context

The ideal society should be affluent and based on a market economy, so that human beings, and more especially women, can be seen and used as commodities. But, despite its affluence, it should also be inequitable in its distribution of wealth and material goods. The inferior status of women should be taken for granted, even in the face of widespread protestations to the contrary, both from women themselves and from those in power. A society where their inferior status remains unquestioned is not good enough: there must be a degree of hypocrisy involved. For instance, societies where women are used as barter, agricultural laborers, or prized solely for their childbearing capacities, will not do. The perfect society is one in which women are granted more or less equal opportunities in theory, but in practice and through series of pressures, some more subtle than others, denied the right to fulfill them. Their skills and talents (especially those of a select few) should be encouraged, but at the same time they must be made to feel that they are less than women if they fail to recognize that their prime function in life is to act as helpmeet to some man, either in the home, the factory or the office, and to bear and nurture children. Only in this context will the right sort of offspring be produced.

2 The Birth of a Daughter

The offspring in question should be a daughter. Male children being prized on the whole above female ones, the birth should be greeted with disappointment, which may be expressed either openly or covertly, or even remain unexpressed in any sort of conscious terms. However, in this last eventuality, the unconscious should be allowed to do its work and express itself in actions rather than in words. These actions should be directed towards an emphasis on the child's intelligence and her ability to succeed, especially at the expense of others, in a competitive world. It should be made clear that high standards of achievement are expected from her, and that anything less than the highest will be received by the parents in an injured fashion as a deliberate act of ingratitude and a blow to the family self-esteem.

3 The Birth of Siblings

Siblings are not essential to this recipe, but they can add spice. They should preferably be younger and of the same sex as the future anorexic. The mother should see to it that the elder child is not "spoiled": basic physical needs should be scrupulously catered to, but infantile emotional demands should be regarded as of secondary importance and as far as possible ignored or quashed. The birth of another child within a year or two can greatly facilitate this task. The elder child's ensuing jealousy can then be exacerbated in two ways: it can be made a family joke, accompanied by some none-too-gentle teasing; or it can be utilized in getting the child to help the mother in ministering to the new arrival, whose needs are paramount. Either of these methods will work, but obviously they will prove more effective when used in conjunction. The aim is to make the child realize that she is not uniquely placed, and that it is necessary for her to subordinate her own needs to those of others. After all, she does not know what her true needs are. She should be told, verbally or by implication, that her selfishness will make her a bad person who deserves to be punished, and it should be hinted that the punishment will take the form of withdrawal of affection on the part of the parents. But if she is a good girl, that is, if she does as they say, she will never be replaced in their affections, which will then remain constant. If the child is unable to tell, by this time, whether she is good or bad, she will get the message, take it to heart, and begin to lose touch with her own real needs.

4 The Family Structure

The family should be a nuclear one, although aunts and grandmothers can be included to contribute to a dominant female presence within the structure. It should be both tight-knit and exclusive. As far as possible, the traditional roles of mother, father, child, should be preserved and any deviation from them regarded as verging upon the criminal. All family rules, no matter to what extent they conflict with those encountered in the larger world outside, should be observed strictly and without question. Mother and father should present a united front at all times, despite hints given to their children that each one is prepared to ally with them against the other. When a child demands a decision from either parent, she should be referred to the other—back and forth several times, if necessary. The usefulness of this behavior lies in its confusing implications: that each parent is willing to go along with whatever decision is made by the other; and the fact that no decisions are actually being made. Respectability should be the parents' watch-word. Disagreements should be rare, and when they do occur, become diffused in circular arguments tinged with self-righteousness, and never culminate in open rows. The aim here is to put across the notion that a happy marriage, like a happy family, is one in which destructive emotions like anger are not and cannot be expressed.

Conformity, too, is important. Parents should make it clear from the outset that their children are their possessions, extensions of themselves, and on whose behavior and achievements they will be judged by neighbors or relatives. In order to instill this notion more firmly, parents should talk about their children in the third person when the child in question is actually present, commenting freely on her physical and characterological traits, and comparing them to those of others in the extended family network. A little friendly argument between parents in such assessments should prove helpful, especially and most directly in the discussion of their growing daughter's weight. But, once any attributions have been made, they should be maintained; each parent should insist that that is her/his story and that she/he is sticking to it.

But these, no matter how confusing they may be to the child, are minor areas of disagreement. All in all, the family too should present a united front to the outside world: it is a cohesive unit—a fact which somehow gives it moral rectitude. The validity of extra-familial friendships should be denied, and the girl accused of preferring the company of her peers to that of her family despite the fact that blood is thicker than water. In this context, ridicule can be a powerful weapon. Whatever may happen in other families—divorce, marital infidelity, juvenile crime, alcoholism or drug addiction, teenage pregnancy, etc.—should, if mentioned at all, be condemned firmly with an air of superiority, and then dismissed as unsuitable subjects for conversation. Such blinkered attitudes in the face of all facts can be more easily fostered when the family is one in which the parents come from cultural or social milieus at variance with the one in which they are now placed, and in which their daughter has to live.

5 The Mother

The mother's attitude to her own role in the family should, like her attitude to her daughter, be essentially ambivalent. She should not work full-time outside the family home, but profess and demonstrate devotion to it, her husband and her children. They constitute her life. At the same time, however, she should make it clear that she is by no means satisfied with that life. The odd, bitter, seemingly casual remark, offered as an aside to her daughter in the absence of the father, is helpful in this context, especially when it reveals a fear or distaste for sexual activity or childbirth. Equally effective is a demand for perfection as regards tidiness in the home, and for an orderliness which includes punctually served meals at which every member of the family must eat every scrap placed in front of her/him: refusal to do so will be taken as rejection, not only of food, but of the mother herself. Thus she can demonstrate both her strength and her vulnerability or, in total, her power. When all else fails, she can resort to illness, especially of the psychosomatic variety, during which the roles of mother and daughter are reversed, and the daughter has to take responsibility for both mother and household. This is an effective strategy for gaining the daughter's sympathy, while at the same time showing her just what sort of life the mother (and therefore all women) normally has to put up with.

The mother should imply that the relationship between herself and her daughter is one of mutual concern, but whereas the concern of the mother is unfailing and beyond criticism, that of the daughter is inadequate and subject to constant (preferably veiled) criticism. Her attitude to her daughter's appearance should reflect this ambivalent attitude, and be given increasing emphasis as the girl grows older. She should sigh about it, but show determination to help the girl "make the most of herself," and choose clothes for her which will hide her "figure faults." If the growing girl is slim, the mother should insist on feeding her up and watch her eat large platefuls of food, while she herself consumes practically nothing. The smoking of cigarettes during such sessions will provide the girl with an added incentive to fulfill the requirements of this recipe.

If the girl is overweight, the mother should not fail to draw attention to the fact, and can deal with it in various ways. She can refer to the surplus weight as puppy-fat and insist that her daughter continue to overeat in order to gain proper nourishment. Or she can put the daughter on a diet, while she herself consumes large amounts of fattening foods. If she chooses this strategy, she should emphasize that boys/men find fat girls/women unattractive. The girl will then wonder why the mother is seemingly unworried about being fat herself. This circumstance provides an excellent opportunity for stressing the importance of finding a male partner, while at the same time describing the male of the species as a predatory beast. The exact nature of his beastliness should never be revealed, just as the details of sexual relations and psychosexual development should never be made explicit. As a third choice, mother and daughter can diet together—a useful activity for revealing the undeclared competition between them. In all, the mother should justify her control of her daughter's life by claiming that she, as the guardian of feminine mysteries, is acting in the girl's best interests, and is at all times her best friend.

6 *The Father*

The father should either be more remote or less powerful than the mother. The two are not necessarily compatible, but in some families where the traditional male/female stereotypes are adhered to, they can be fitted together quite easily and, indeed, the combination will produce better results. The father can present himself as someone absorbed in his own work outside the home, to the exclusion of a similar involvement in what goes on within it. The latter is the mother's sphere of operation. He should take a pride in his family and in being its breadwinner, but at the same time air his financial worries and complain about the burden of his greater responsibility in the presence of his wife and children, who are all incapable of understanding its mysteries. If he is absent from home, or emotionally absent though physically present, it is because he has to work, or has had to work, *for their benefit.* This is an effective strategy for various reasons.

First, he can still insist that his primary loyalty is to the family which he consistently neglects in emotional, that is, primary terms. The second reason, which follows from the first, is that his children will be more aware of his absence than of its possible long-term beneficial effects. Third, his absence can be used by him as an excuse for opting out of decision-making. But it must be made clear by both himself and his wife that he is the ultimate authority, however weak and vacillating he may appear, and has power to lay down the law from above or from afar. For this reason alone, his daughter should learn to respect and even revere him. His attitude to her can be either indulgent or tyrannical or, preferably, each in turn so that she never knows when she is going to be praised or blamed. He should take a critical interest in her scholastic achievements and in other skills which she can demonstrate to his satisfaction within a competitive environment, but little or none in her emotional life. Ideally, he should be vague and ineffectual in his management of personal relationships, but able to rise to the occasion and bluster or bully when called upon to do so by his wife.

7 The School

For the purpose of this recipe, the school can be called upon to replace some of the other ingredients, such as father (but probably not mother) and family structure. But it is best that they should all be mixed in together. Single-sex schools are preferable to mixed ones, and boarding-schools to day-schools. It is also better that the school should work on a selective rather than a comprehensive basis. A single-sex school will help to ensure that the girl has few dealings with boys of her own age: they will remain a separate species with whom she is not in academic competition. A boarding-school will serve to reinforce this situation, and can present added advantages. It should, like the home, be a rigid structure which affords little opportunity for autonomy. If the rigidity demands a form of conduct which is different from or in active conflict with that demanded in the home, so much the better. If the move from home to school involves upward social mobility, better still: it will then be ensured that the girl, as an adolescent in need of some coherent structure necessary for growth, or for the general development of her personality, will become so torn by conflicting loyalties that she will be unable to move in any direction, and so unable to grow.

8 The Female Body

From earliest childhood onwards, the girl should be constantly fed with messages about the female body. Parents, teachers, doctors, should emphasize its inadequacies in general, while making it clear at the same time that female anatomy constitutes female destiny. Its primary physiological functions should not, however, be discussed in detail, especially where these differ from those of the male body. The import of these messages should be that the female body is a cross to bear, and that its mysteries are unspeakable. As the girl grows older, advertising and the media will present her with differing messages: that the female body is a source of gratification, and exists to be used for that purpose; that it has the power to ensnare, which is perhaps the only real power available to women; and that there is such a thing as an "ideal" body, with an "ideal" weight and "ideal" measurements. Such messages should be ubiquitous. They should conflict with what she has been told already about her body, and will reflect the generally ambivalent attitude towards the role of women in her particular society. The more they contradict earlier received information, and the more they contradict one another, the better.

This recipe represents an extreme case, and one which tallies less perhaps with my own experience than with the anorexic picture in general. It is, of course, a recipe for the creation of psychoneurosis in general, and can be applied to anorexia nervosa in particular where it refers to the position of women and to notions about the female body. Its concern is with prevention rather than cure, and I have put the case for prevention negatively simply because I don't see how it can be put positively. Human affairs are characterized by imponderables, even when certain patterns emerge from certain chains of events. In either a perfect or a poverty-stricken society, anorexia nervosa would not exist. But a perfect society is an impossibility for reasons which are as much historical as ontological: we inherit the imperfections of the past, as our parents did before us. And a poverty-stricken society is, except as far as a handful of atavistic idealists is concerned, an undesirable one. All that can be done is to identify the possible predisposing factors in the disease, and then attempt to avoid or emend them. Easier said than done, I know.

Just as there can be no such thing as a perfect society, so there can be no such thing as perfect parenting: at best there can only be what

Winnicott calls "good enough" parenting. It would be nice to say that such parenting is a matter of common sense—as indeed it is—and leave it at that. But common sense is a rarer commodity than is often supposed. If a mother or father is unfortunate enough to feel continually anxious, depressed, frustrated, or trapped within an unhappy marriage, such feelings will communicate themselves to the children, however conscientiously suppressed. And to expect unwavering common sense in such circumstances is to demand the impossible or, perhaps, the inhuman. It is interesting, though, to note that both mothers and fathers of anorexics tend to suppress conflict either within themselves or within the family, and to pride themselves on being conscientious parents. It is as though being "good enough" were not good enough for them—for whatever personal reasons. And so, in attempting to be more than "good enough," they become "too good to be true," or seemingly unassailable. The falsity of their position will be apparent to the anorexic.

It is, I think, no accident that anorexic behavior parallels such contradictions in parental behavior and converts them into paradoxes. Children learn less by precept than they do by example, and if the examples with which they are confronted embody a large amount of contradiction, it is hardly surprising that they in turn will adopt similarly contradictory behavior. As already stated, anorexics attempt to deny feelings of helplessness and hopelessness by seeking after an impossible perfection. Like their parents (and perhaps grandparents and great-grandparents before them) they can never be "good enough" people, and so must set themselves up as being supremely "good"—in whatever area, but most especially in the area of self-control. Anorexics are not created deliberately, but by default. In the bluntest of terms, my advice to parents who wish to avoid any such creation would be: stop worrying about being perfect, and concentrate on being human instead. Or: what you perceptibly are is more valuable to yourself and others than what you profess to be, more important than what you may or may not have achieved. And the same applies to your daughter—a person who is both *female* and *autonomous*. The two qualities are not at variance, whatever your own experience or wider social pressures may tell you to the contrary. Indeed, they may even be mutually enhancing.

My recipe for the creation of an anorexic is much too comprehensive to be applied to any given individual case. It is a generalized picture which attempts to include the multiplicity of predisposing factors. If it reads bitterly, that bitterness should not be interpreted as an attack upon parents (least of all my own) but upon the elusive and complex forces which compel basically well-intentioned people to act against both their own and their children's best interests. In a sense, we are all victims. Equally, we are all less sensitive than we might be to the needs of others. According to received wisdom, the Golden Rule of human conduct is: doing unto others as we would want them to do unto us. According to Szasz,[2] there are two other major ethical modes. First, "The Rule of Respect: doing unto others as they would want us to do unto them." And, "The Rule of Paternalism: doing unto them in their own best interests." I would submit that the parents of anorexics, while subscribing in theory to the Golden Rule, operate in practice according to the Rule of Paternalism and never approach an understanding of the Rule of Respect as far as their own growing-up children are concerned. Their failure to do so cannot be castigated as a crime, but although it may spring from the best of (anxiety-ridden) motives, it is nevertheless a shortcoming. And on this point I must allow Szasz to have the last word: "Three R's: Reciprocity. Respect. Responsibility. The three pillars of the ethics of autonomy." The inferences to be drawn with regard to anorexia nervosa are surely too obvious to need spelling out.

If my list of predisposing factors seems to adhere to "confusion theory," as outlined in Chapter 6, then the precipitating factors can be seen as belonging to "defense theory." They are what make the confused worm turn. Dally lists five of them, but fails to give enough emphasis to what is for many anorexics the main factor: that of the onset of puberty or menarche. It is then that a girl with the right predisposition will be most likely to rebel against what is happening to her. Even if there is an interval of a few years between the start of menstruation and the onset of anorexia nervosa, I would still list it as one of the primary precipitating factors.

Dally's list of possibilities starts with a fear of fatness, which he connects with a fear of womanhood and sexuality. I would accept this as far as it goes, but he fails to make a direct connection between any such fear and the almost inevitable increase in body weight, along with other bodily changes, which accompany or follow on from menarche. The second item or event on the list is the death or serious illness of a close relative, which can lead to the release of suppressed aggressive feelings, guilt and remorse on the part of the pre-anorexic. The third is an illness suffered by the girl herself. The fourth is some sort of failure at school or work. This can be a failure in real, that is, objectively acceptable terms, but it is more likely to be imagined and exist only within the girl's own over-anxious mind. The fifth is described as sexual conflicts, which can either be direct or indirect, but serve in each case to bring suppressed fears to the surface. Those directly involving the girl herself can range from menstruation (only briefly mentioned) to the hearing or overhearing of a "dirty story." Those involving others can include a sister's or friend's marriage or pregnancy, and the remarriage of a parent. I find all these possibilities substantially correct, given the predisposing factors already outlined. But I should like to add that a feeling of helplessness and hopelessness can in itself be a precipitating factor. In other words, there is no necessity for a last straw, because the pre-anorexic girl may have already experienced what seems to her like a series of last straws, each one more unbearable and more incredible than the one before it. Sometimes there is one identifiable precipitating factor; sometimes the precipitating factor is the sum total of her life itself.

Anorexia nervosa is fostered by ignorance and insensitivity displayed by the adult population in their dealings with female children and adolescents. The acquisition of knowledge and sensitivity may influence parents and other closely-involved adults, who are on the whole (despite my extreme recipe) caring people with problems of their own. But it is unlikely to have much effect on commercial enterprise or prevalent sexist prejudice, which are both exercises in power, the former being cynically manipulative and the latter desperately entrenched. We cannot expect a sensitive or sympathetic response from such sources. However, I believe that an awareness of the individual's true needs within the immediate community of caring adults can outweigh such adverse attitudes. And an awareness of the adverse attitudes themselves, with all their implications, can lead to a more sensitive handling of the problems a girl or young woman faces in coming to terms with her being-in-the-world. In more practical terms, the advice given to parents by the Anorexia Counselling Service includes the recommendations,

> that they do *not* try to feed or weigh their daughter (her body is *her* concern); that they do not label her as ill, or treat her like a helpless child; that they discuss her problems and feelings in an open, accepting way; that they encourage her to take responsibility for herself, without making a moral issue of it; that they help her love and accept herself; that they allow and encourage her to make her own decisions; and that they are not neurotic about their own eating and body weight.[3]

Again, perhaps, easier said than done. But it is at the same time excellent advice.

Turning then from prevention to cure, we are forced to accept that the latter involves a process of undoing, which must necessarily be long and slow, probably painful for all concerned, and maybe even at best only partial. The aims are to save lives and to alleviate unhappiness, but to save a life is easier than to make that saved life acceptable to the individual who has to live it. This is not a medical problem to which organic or mechanistic means can be applied, but a social, psychological, and even philosophical one. As the epigraph to his recent book, *The Myth of Psychotherapy*, Szasz quotes Joseph Conrad: "Strictly speaking, the question is not how to get cured, but how to live."[4] An anorexic is not simply a girl or young woman who doesn't eat and can be considered cured when she resumes eating. She is someone who doesn't know how to live except by non-eating. The fact that she cannot otherwise come to terms with her own life expresses a contradiction, in that non-eating leads to illness and eventually to death; and it expresses a paradox in that her apparent choice of death is in reality a bid for life. Any attempt at cure must involve the resolution of both contradiction and paradox. The means to effecting any such resolutions will depend on the needs of the individual anorexic, and be assessed according to her age and the length of her illness, as well as to other peculiar circumstances of her own case.

To describe anorexia nervosa solely as the result of a capitalist or male-chauvinist plot is as unhelpful as to describe it solely as the result of traumas experienced in early childhood, or solely as a medical problem. The complexity of the factors involved in the aetiology of the disease does not allow for a simplistic approach to its alleviation. In order to change complex conditions, complex measures are required. And, as in all psychosomatic disorders, the success of those measures will depend very largely on the sympathy and understanding of those prepared to undertake them. It may seem superfluous to add that the anorexic should at all times be treated as an individual and independent human being but, in the face of the many wrong-headed and even damaging forms of treatment which are still being practiced in England and elsewhere, I feel it is a demand which cannot be overstated.

NOTES

INTRODUCTION

1. A. H. Crisp, R. L. Palmer and R. S. Kalucy, "How Common Is Anorexia Nervosa? A Prevalence Study," *British Journal of Psychiatry*, 1976, 128, 549–54. New York: Center for the Study of Anorexia, 1981.

2. Joan E. Martin, "Anorexia Nervosa. A Disorder of Weight," *Occupational Therapy*, September 1978.

3. Crisp *et al.*, *op. cit.*

4. E. L. Bliss and C. H. H. Branch, *Anorexia Nervosa*, New York: Harper & Row, 1960.

CHAPTER 1 GENERAL HISTORY

1. Sigmund Freud, *The Standard Edition of the Complete Psychological Works of Sigmund Freud*, Vol I, p. 242, Letter to Wilhelm Fliess, 17.1. 1897.

2. Thomas S. Szasz, *The Manufacture of Madness*, New York: Harper & Row, 1977.

3. Barbara Ehrenreich and Deirdre English, *For Her Own Good. 150 Years of the Experts' Advice to Women*, New York: Doubleday, 1979.

4. M. Boss, *Einfuehrung in die Psychosomatische Medizin*, Huber, 1954.

5. Mara Selvini Palazzoli, *Self-Starvation. From the Intrapsychic to the Transpersonal Approach to Anorexia Nervosa*, New York: Aronson, 1978.

6. H. Binswanger, "The Case of Ellen West," quoted in Rollo May *et al.*, *Existence*, New York: Basic Books, 1959.

7. Peter Dally, *Anorexia Nervosa*, New York: Grune & Stratton, 1969.

8. Quoted in *ibid.*

9. Hilde Bruch, *Eating Disorders. Obesity, Anorexia Nervosa and the Person Within*, New York: Basic Books, 1973 (text), 1979 (paperback).

10. Joan E. Martin, "Anorexia Nervosa. A Disorder of Weight," *Occupational Therapy*, September 1978.

11. A. J. Stunkard *et al.*, "Behaviour Therapy of Anorexia Nervosa; Effectiveness of Activity as a Reinforcer of Weight Gain," *American Journal of Psychiatry*, 1970, 126, 77–82.

12. Selvini Palazzoli, *op. cit.*

13. Salvador Minuchin, Bernice L. Rosman and Lester Baker, *Psychosomatic Families. Anorexia Nervosa in Context*, Cambridge, Mass.: Harvard University Press, 1978.

14. W. H. Auden, *A Certain World*, New York: Viking, 1970.

15. Ehrenreich and English, *op. cit.*

CHAPTER 2 BACKGROUND

1. Theodore Lidz, "Hamlet's Enemy," *Madness and Myth in Hamlet*, London: Vision Press, 1975.

2. Morton Schatzman, *Soul Murder. Persecution in the Family*, New York: New American Library, 1974.

3. *Ibid.*

4. Salvador Minuchin *et al.*, *Psychosomatic Families. Anorexia Nervosa in Context*, Cambridge, Mass.: Harvard University Press, 1978.

5. A. H. Crisp *et al.*, "How Common Is Anorexia Nervosa? A Prevalence Study," *British Journal of Psychiatry*, 1976, 128, 549–54.

6. R. D. Laing and A. Esterson, *Sanity, Madness and the Family*, New York: Penguin, 1970.

7. Thomas S. Szasz, *The Second Sin*, New York: Doubleday, 1973.

8. *Ibid.*

9. Hilde Bruch, *The Golden Cage: The Enigma of Anorexia Nervosa*, Cambridge, Mass.: Harvard University Press, 1978; New York: Random House, 1979.

10. Karl Menninger, *Love Against Hate*, New York: Harcourt, Brace & Co., 1942.

11. Elias Canetti, *Crowds and Power*, New York: Continuum, 1978.

12. D. W. Winnicott. *Playing and Reality*, New York: Basic Books, 1971.

13. *Ibid.*
14. Hilde Bruch, *Eating Disorders. Obesity, Anorexia Nervosa and the Person Within*, New York: Basic Books, 1973 (text), 1979 (paperback).
15. Minuchin *et al.*, *op. cit.*
16. Erik H. Erikson, *Identity: Youth and Crisis*, New York: Norton, 1968.

CHAPTER 3 ONSET

1. Hilde Bruch, *The Golden Cage: The Enigma of Anorexia Nervosa*, Cambridge, Mass.: Harvard University Press, 1978; New York: Random House, 1979.
2. Hilde Bruch, *Eating Disorders. Obesity, Anorexia Nervosa and the Person Within*, New York: Basic Books, 1973 (text), 1979 (paperback).
3. Mara Selvini Palazzoli, *Self-Starvation. From the Intrapsychic to the Transpersonal Approach to Anorexia Nervosa*, New York: Aronson, 1978.
4. Ruth Benedict, *Patterns of Culture*, Boston: Houghton Mifflin, 1934.
5. W. H. Auden, *The Dyer's Hand*, New York: Random House, 1968.
6. Erik H. Erikson, *Identity: Youth and Crisis*, New York: Norton, 1968.
7. Morton Schatzman, *Soul Murder. Persecution in the Family*, New York: New American Library, 1974.
8. *Ibid.*
9. Erich Fromm, *The Anatomy of Human Destructiveness*, New York: Holt, Rinehart & Winston, 1973.
10. Jules Henry, *Culture Against Man*, New York: Random House, 1965.
11. Salvador Minuchin *et al.*, *Psychosomatic Families. Anorexia Nervosa in Context*, Cambridge, Mass.: Harvard University Press, 1978.
12. Liam Hudson, *Frames of Mind*, London: Methuen, 1968.
13. Rollo May, *Power and Innocence. A Search for the Sources of Violence*, New York: Norton, 1972.
14. Erikson, *op. cit.*

CHAPTER 4 EUPHORIA

1. Erik H. Erikson, *Identity: Youth and Crisis*, New York: Norton, 1968.
2. *Ibid.*
3. Erik H. Erikson, *Childhood and Society*, New York: Norton, 1964.
4. *Ibid.*
5. Thomas S. Szasz, *The Second Sin*, New York: Doubleday, 1973.

6. *Ibid.*

7. Michael Polanyi, *Knowing and Being*, Chicago: University of Chicago Press, 1969.

8. Sigmund Freud and Joseph Breuer, *Studies on Hysteria*, London: Penguin, 1974.

9. W. R. D. Fairbairn, "Observations on the Nature of Hysterical States," *British Journal Medical Psychology*, 1954, 27:05.

10. Thomas S. Szasz, *The Myth of Mental Illness*, New York: Harper & Row, 1974.

11. Carl Gustav Jung, *Memories. Dreams. Reflections*, New York: Random House, 1965.

12. Norman N. Holland, *Five Readers Reading*, New Haven: Yale University Press, 1975.

13. Mara Selvini Palazzoli, *Self-Starvation. From the Intrapsychic to the Transpersonal Approach to Anorexia Nervosa*, New York: Aronson, 1978.

14. Carl Gustav Jung, *Modern Man in Search of a Soul*, New York: Harcourt, 1955.

15. Thomas S. Szasz, *The Myth of Mental Illness.*

16. Selvini Palazzoli, *op. cit.*

17. Alfred Adler, quotes in J. A. C. Brown, *Freud and the Post-Freudians*, Baltimore: Penguin, 1961.

CHAPTER 5 DEPRESSION

1. Peter Dally, *Anorexia Nervosa*, New York: Grune & Stratton, 1969.

2. Hilde Bruch, *Eating Disorders. Obesity, Anorexia Nervosa and the Person Within*, New York: Basic Books, 1973 (text), 1979 (paperback).

3. Leslie H. Farber, *The Ways of the Will*, New York: Harper & Row, 1974.

4. Sylvia Plath, *Ariel*, New York: Harper & Row, 1968.

5. E. S. Shneidman and N. L. Farberow, "Suicide and Death" in Herman Feifel (ed.), *The Meaning of Death*, New York: McGraw-Hill, 1959.

6. Morton Schatzman, *Soul Murder. Persecution in the Family*, New York: New American Library, 1974.

7. Shneidman and Farberow, *op. cit.*

8. Farber, *op. cit.*

9. Bruch, *op. cit.*

10. Mara Selvini Palazzoli, *Self-Starvation. From the Intrapsychic to the Transpersonal Approach to Anorexia Nervosa*, New York: Aronson, 1978.

11. Erich Fromm, *The Dogma of Christ*, "Sex and Character," New York: Holt, Rinehart & Winston, 1963.

12. Erik H. Erikson, *Childhood and Society*, New York: Norton, 1964.

13. Selvini Palazzoli, *op. cit.*

14. Peter Lomas, *True and False Experience*, New York: Taplinger, 1973.

15. Sheila MacLeod, *The Snow-White Soliloquies*, London: Secker & Warbug, 1970.

16. Bruch, *op. cit.*

17. Farber, *op. cit.*

CHAPTER 6 RECOVERY

1. Mara Selvini Palazzoli, *Self-Starvation. From the Intrapsychic to the Transpersonal Approach to Anorexia Nervosa*, New York: Aronson, 1978.

2. Katherina Havekamp, *Love Comes in Buckets*, London: Marion Boyars, 1978.

3. Hilde Bruch, *Eating Disorders. Obesity, Anorexia Nervosa and the Person Within*, New York: Basic Books, 1973 (text), 1979 (paperback).

4. William Blake, "The Sunflower" in Geoffrey Keynes (ed.), *Complete Writing*, New York: Oxford University Press, 1966.

5. Salvador Minuchin *et al.*, *Psychosomatic Families. Anorexia Nervosa in Context*, Cambridge, Mass.: Harvard University Press, 1978.

6. *Ibid.*

7. May Duddle, "An Increase of Anorexia Nervosa in a University Population," *British Journal of Psychiatry*, 1973, 123, 711–12.

8. Selvini Palazzoli, *op. cit.*

9. *Ibid.*

10. *Ibid.*

11. Erik H. Erikson, *Childhood and Society*, New York: Norton, 1964.

12. Bruch, *op. cit.*

13. Bruch, *op. cit.*

14. Peter Lomas, *True and False Experience*, New York: Taplinger, 1973.

15. Selvini Palazzoli, *op. cit.*

16. Viktor Frankl, *The Doctor and the Soul*, New York: Random House, 1973.

17. Lomas, *op. cit.*

18. Selvini Palazzoli, *op. cit.*

19. Bruch, *op. cit.*

20. Anorexic Aid, Gravel House, Copthall Corner, Chalfont St Peter, Bucks, England.

21. Leslie H. Farber, *The Ways of the Will*, New York: Harper & Row, 1974.

22. Marilyn Lawrence and Celia Lowenstein, "Self-Starvation," *Spare Rib*, May 1979.

CHAPTER 7 PROGNOSIS

1. Peter Dally, *Anorexia Nervosa*, New York: Grune & Stratton, 1969.

2. Mara Selvini Palazzoli, *Self-Starvation. From the Intrapsychic to the Transpersonal Approach to Anorexia Nervosa*, New York: Aronson, 1978.

3. Jean-Paul Sartre, *Words*, New York: Random House, 1981.

4. Dally, *op. cit.*

5. Hilde Bruch, *Eating Disorders. Obesity, Anorexia Nervosa and the Person Within*, New York: Basic Books, 1973 (text), 1979 (paperback).

6. Selvini Palazzoli, *op. cit.*

7. E. Le Roy Ladurie, *The History of the Historian*, "Amenorrhoea in a Time of Famine," Brighton: Harvester Press, 1979.

8. Penelope Shuttle and Peter Redgrove, *The Wise Wound*, New York: Marek, 1978.

9. Salvador Minuchin *et al.*, *Psychosomatic Families. Anorexia Nervosa in Context*, Cambridge, Mass.: Harvard University Press, 1978.

10. Selvini Palazzoli, *op. cit.*

11. A. H. Crisp *et al.*, "How Common Is Anorexia Nervosa? A Prevalence Study," *British Journal of Psychiatry*, 1976, 128, 549–54.

12. May Duddle, "An Increase of Anorexia Nervosa in a University Population," *British Journal of Psychiatry*, 1973, 123, 711–12.

13. Marilyn Lawrence and G. Edwards, Information leaflet prepared for BBC 2 TV programme, *Grapevine*, shown May and June 1979.

14. Crisp *et al.*, *op. cit.*

15. Dally, *op. cit.*

16. J. Kellett, M. Trimble and A. Thorley, "Anorexia Nervosa After the Menopause," *British Journal of Psychiatry*, 1976, 128, 555–58.

17. Lawrence and Edwards, *op. cit.*

CHAPTER 8 CONCLUSIONS

1. Peter Dally, *Anorexia Nervosa*, New York: Grune & Stratton, 1969.

2. Thomas S. Szasz, *The Second Sin*, New York: Doubleday, 1973.

3. Marilyn Lawrence and G. Edwards, Information leaflet prepared for BBC 2 TV programme, *Grapevine*, shown May and June 1979.

4. Thomas S. Szasz, *The Myth of Psychotherapy*, New York: Anchor/ Doubleday, 1979.